Friendship and Literature

SPIRIT AND FORM

Ronald A. Sharp

Duke University Press

Durham 1986

© 1986 Duke University Press
All rights reserved
Printed in the United States of America on acid-free paper ∞
Library of Congress Cataloging-in-Publication data
appear on the last printed page of this book

Permission to quote from the following selections is gratefully acknowledged.

W. H. Auden: "For Friends Only" and "Tonight at Seven-Thirty," in *About the House,* © 1965 by Random House, Inc. Reprinted by permission of Random House, Inc.

Emily Dickinson: "The Day She Goes" and "Her Breast Is Fit for Pearls," in *The Poems of Emily Dickinson,* ed. Thomas H. Johnson, Cambridge, Mass.: The Belknap Press of Harvard University Press, copyright 1951, © 1955, 1979, 1983 by the President and Fellows of Harvard College. Reprinted by permission of Harvard University Press.

Arthur Kirsch: unpublished paper on *The Merchant of Venice.* Reprinted by permission of the author.

Ezra Pound: "Exile's Letter" and "Taking Leave of a Friend," in *Personae: The Collected Shorter Poems,* copyright 1926 by Ezra Pound. Reprinted by permission of New Directions Publishing Corporation (New York) and Faber & Faber, Ltd. (England).

Philip Schultz: forthcoming novel *Upstart Crows.* Reprinted by permission of the author.

Walt Whitman: "Earth, My Likeness," "For You O Democracy," "Here the Frailest Leaves of Me," "I Dream'd in a Dream," "I Hear It Was Charged Against Me," and "To the East and to the West," in *The Collected Writings of Walt Whitman,* vol. 9: *Leaves of Grass: Comprehensive Reader's Edition,* ed. Harold W. Blodgett and Sculley Bradley, © 1965 by New York University. Reprinted by permission of New York University Press.

For my mother

In memory of my father

And for my children, Andy and Jimmy

Contents

Acknowledgments vii

Introduction 1

1 Friendship and Form 11

2 Friendship as Gift Exchange 82

3 *The Merchant of Venice* 118

Notes 155

Works Cited 167

Index 177

Acknowledgments

I am happy to acknowledge the advice, criticism, and support of colleagues, students, friends, and family. Wayne Booth, Jim Ceaser, Guy Davenport, Jim Hans, Michael Harper, Ron Presser, George Steiner, Walter Waring, and Jay Wright read the entire manuscript with great care, giving generously not only their time and advice but their encouragement as well. Kenneth Burke warned me about gridlock but urged me on nevertheless, raising a wide range of important questions along the way. I am also indebted to various people who read portions of the manuscript and offered useful suggestions: Paul Cantor, Adele Davidson, Karen Edwards, Robert Hass, Lewis Hyde, Arthur Kirsch, Diana Rhoads, and Steve Rhoads. Barbara Myerhoff read and commented on my first two chapters with her usual insight and charity; before her death last year, we had a number of talks about friendship that, like everything else about this extraordinary person, made a deep and lasting impression on me.

I am especially grateful to the National Endowment for the Humanities, which awarded me three grants related to this book: one to support a year of research and writing and two to conduct summer seminars on the Literature of Friendship for secondary school teachers. Kenyon College has also generously supported my work through Faculty Development grants, through the kind assistance of Bill Dameron, Nadine

George, and the rest of the staff of Chalmers Memorial Library, and above all through its provost, Jerry Irish, who not only took an active interest in this project from its inception, but also read most of the manuscript and offered much valuable advice. I should also like to thank the staff of Alderman Library at the University of Virginia, where I did most of my research. I wish there were space to name each of the students who studied the Literature of Friendship with me at Kenyon. Their questions and responses, along with those of the participants in my NEH seminars, contributed a great deal to the shape of this book.

Among the many other people who have helped in one way or another, I particularly wish to thank M. H. Abrams, Barbara Busenburg, the late Robert Daniel, Martin Esslin, E. D. Hirsch, Jr., Pat Irish, Sheila Jordan, Eleanor Loucks, David Lynn, Michael Moses, Paul Posnak, Mary Sparlin, and Fred Turner.

Reynolds Smith, Joanne Ferguson, Nancy Margolis, and Pam Morrison at Duke University Press shepherded my manuscript to its final form with efficiency, kindness, and sensitivity. I want to thank Betty Herr Hallinger for preparing the index. I also want to acknowledge *Modern Philology,* where parts of my third chapter originally appeared under the title "Gift Exchange and the Economies of Spirit in *The Merchant of Venice.*"

I come, finally, to my family—to my mother, my father (who died while I was writing this book), my brother, my wife, and my two children. I am, of course, grateful for their patience and understanding, for their encouragement and advice while I was working on this project. But in a book like this, in which the connections between friendship and love are obvious, I feel their gift throughout.

Introduction

"What is friendship, that it should have such power? Everyone knows about love. Romantic love, married love, adulterous love: happy love affairs, unhappy ones. Everyone knows about *love,* no one knows about *friendship.*"—Judith, in Joyce Carol Oates's "Love. Friendship"

One night about seven years ago my wife and I returned home from a party to find our baby-sitter looking utterly confused. A few hours earlier she had put our two-year-old boy Andy to sleep and then been summoned back to his room to "take out Bibi, Brian, Bouch, Sammy, and Giant."

"Who?" she asked him.

"Bibi, Brian, Bouch, Sammy, and Giant."

Two-year-olds do not talk much, even to teenage baby-sitters, so after numerous fruitless inquiries she moved out every stuffed animal in the room, one at a time. He still was not satisfied.

"Bibi," Andy told her; "not the animals. Bibi and the others."

After moving out his rocking horse, a chair, a table, and a small bookcase, she gave up.

"Who," she now demanded of us, "Who in the world is Bibi and Giant and Brock?"

"Bouch," I said.

"What?"

"Bouch," I said. "It's Bouch, not Brock. The pronunciation is very important. The *ch* has to come from the back of your throat. I think it's somehow derived from *ba-ruch,* the first word of some Hebrew prayers he'd heard. Giant? Giant's . . ."

The sitter cut me off and I drove her home.

Coming upon this anecdote at the opening of a book about friendship will make clear what remained mysterious to the baby-sitter: Bibi and Co. were my son's imaginary friends. As with many children, these creatures simply appeared in his young life at a certain point, their names emerging from bits of his experience: Sammy is the name of a friend's cat; Brian is the name of one of my own childhood friends about whom I had recently told Andy stories; Giant is the word I used to describe the fruit that had just appeared on our peach tree; only Bibi remains a mystery. The significance of imaginary friends in the development of children is itself a fascinating subject, but I raise it here only to remind us at the outset of the remarkable power of friendship in our lives. So fundamental is that presence that the leading anthropological study of friendship, Robert Brain's *Friends and Lovers,* refers to it as "a universal characteristic of human society" (20). Though it takes different forms in different cultures, "research has shown," says Brain, "that no culture fails to laud the undivided loyalty and selfless love of friends" (18).

There is something ingenuous about that phrase, "research has shown," but not quite as ingenuous as the remark attributed to the infamous Yorkshire killer, heir to Jack the Ripper, who apparently left a note with one of his victims quoting a popular song: "I want to thank you for being a friend." However universal friendship may be, it is something else again to take up the subject in a culture in which a recent best-seller was called *How to Be Your Own Best Friend,* or in which a recent television commercial showed a man relieved of the agonies of hemorrhoids, able, at last, to relate to his family and be productive at work, smiling into the camera and telling millions of viewers that Preparation H is his "good friend."

When Meursault, the hero of Camus's *The Stranger,* is asked by his girlfriend Marie if he would marry her, his reaction is, "I didn't mind; if she was keen on it, we'd get married. Then she asked me again if I loved her. I replied, much as before, that her question meant nothing or next to nothing—but I supposed I didn't" (52). When Raymond, his neighbor, calls on him for help, he obliges, and Raymond tells him, " 'I'll be your pal for life. . . .' When I [Meursault] made no comment, he asked me if I'd like us to be pals. I replied that I had no objection, and that appeared to satisfy him" (36). Later, Raymond slaps him on the shoulder, calls him "old boy," and says, " 'So now we're pals, ain't we?' I kept silence," says Meursault, "and he said it again. I didn't care one way or the other; but as he seemed so set on it, I nodded and said, 'Yes' " (41).

Meursault moves through his existence anesthetized by his sense of absurdity and meaninglessness, and unable, therefore, to regard any human relationship—including love and friendship—as more than a tissue of convention into which and out of which one simply drifts. The promise of intimacy is to him a mere delusion.

As a figure of modern loneliness, a man alienated from the deepest and most nourishing rhythms and values of human fellowship, Meursault takes his place alongside Kafka's Gregor Samsa and Eliot's Prufrock. Gregor, the antihero of *The Metamorphosis,* has a few "casual acquaintances" but they are "always new and never become intimate friends" (68). Prufrock, imagining himself "pinned and wriggling on the wall" (58), an insect fixed by his acquaintances' glares "in a formulated phrase" (56), may be more vulnerable than Meursault and Gregor, but he shares with them a characteristically modern friendlessness that is profoundly connected to loneliness:

> There will be time, there will be time
> To prepare a face to meet the faces that you meet.
> (26–27)

Any college sophomore can recite the litany of loneliness and alienation that characterizes so much of the twentieth century and is reflected in much of its literature and art: from the utter failure of communication and intimacy in the theater of the absurd to the radical paranoia in the novels of Pynchon; from the spare and dwindled sculptured figures of Giacometti to the latest hollow-cheeked and concentration-camp-pale model on the cover of *Vogue.* There can be no doubt that the recent plight of friendship is related to all those elements of modernity that have been variously associated with existential *angst,* narcissism, rootlessness, nihilism, alienation, the breakdown of community, and general estrangement. My purpose here is not to explain the rise of modern loneliness or the decline of the amorphous and undifferentiated spirit of friendliness. Those issues can no more be separated from the situation of friendship than *friend* can be separated from *stranger* as a contrasting set of categories implicit in the title of Camus's novella. My concern in this book lies elsewhere.

We begin with a loud silence. Why is it that there has been so little serious writing about friendship in recent years? Love, sex, and marriage have been the central subjects of a great variety of serious twentieth-century literature, but with very few exceptions, friendship—which up through the nineteenth century remained a major issue for serious writers and philosophers—seems to have fallen mainly into the hands of pop psychologists and self-help enthusiasts. There are, to be sure, recent works about friendship, but, as Wayne Booth has observed, their scarcity and superficiality are remarkable: "The neglect of friendship as a serious subject of inquiry in modern thought is itself a strange and wondrous thing; after millennia during which it was one of the major philosophical topics, the subject of thousands of books and tens of thousands of essays, it has now dwindled to the point that our encyclopedias do not even mention it" (6).[1]

This situation is all the more remarkable when one reflects on the self-consciousness that has for so long accompanied our modern loneliness. For in the face of that painful loneliness, friendship seems to have reemerged as something both highly valued and intensely desired. Particularly as a result of the strains and fractures of the family, friendship seems increasingly to be a key source of support and affection. Many people clearly feel, even if they do not acknowledge, that friendship is central to their lives, and all the more so in a secular age when friendship has increasingly assumed, as I argue later, spiritual functions.

Why, then, have we maintained such stringent economies in both the analysis and the praise of friendship? What is it that accounts for the odd gap between our high regard for friendship and our loud silence about it? Has friendship slipped into an imaginative realm around which, for the time being, some inner cultural necessity has erected barriers against verbal inspection, in order to protect it from a harsh environment?

By "harsh environment" I mean not only the kind of loneliness and alienation that I referred to earlier, or the more public and violent horrors of our time, which likewise affect the climate for friendship. I also mean that major tendency of twentieth-century thought which explains all phenomena—friendship included—by tracing their origins to the genes, the economy, the unconscious, or mere self-interest. These reductive forms of interpretation, which pretend to expose base motives beneath lofty feelings, patronize friendship at best, and discredit it at worst.

The same, unfortunately, is true at the other end of the spectrum. If friendship has had its problems with cynicism, it has had equal problems with sentimentality. Much of friendship's currency in our time has been in the platitudes of warmth and coziness that fill the popular "friendship lines" of greeting cards; in the saccharine and desperate intimacies and dependencies of soap-opera friendships in the glare of daylight; and in the endless parade of buddies playing racquetball before they reach for their Buds or hop into their Toyotas. Friendship also figures prominently in innumerable television dramas and comedies, including perhaps the three best of recent years: *MASH, The Mary Tyler Moore Show,* and *Hill Street Blues.* And we find it everywhere in the movies: *Diner, Julia, The Turning Point, The Front, Gal-*

lipoli, The Four Seasons, Manhattan, The Sting, Butch Cassidy and the Sundance Kid, Tootsie, Autumn Sonata, Kramer vs. Kramer, Kotch, The Deer Hunters, My Dinner with André, The Karate Kid, Breaking Away, The Chosen, The Big Chill, Willy and Phil, Girlfriends, and the *Star Wars* series, to name only a few from the last decade or so. Only in the film, it seems, has friendship been explored in some depth during recent years.

Why it is that friendship has become so peripheral to the modern novel, short story, poetry, theater, and essay, and why it has had such play in television and film is a question as difficult to answer as it is fascinating. But surely the answer has something to do with the fact that television and film have more often had to confront a mass audience than the other forms, and have had to come to terms with the charge of sentimentality. For it has been mainly the popular culture that has had the insight (or the innocence) to take up the great theme of friendship. Not only has recent serious writing largely ignored friendship; most serious readers and intellectuals do not even know which works constitute the long tradition of writing about the subject. It is one thing for there to be a decline in writing about friendship; it is something else again for the canon of writing about it to be virtually lost.

These facts have much to do with our endemic fear of sentimentality, a fear less pardonable, in my view, than the sentimentality of the commercial icons themselves. On this theme, the best lack all conviction. While I was writing this book I was advised time and again to include a chapter on betrayal, to concentrate more on the way friends manipulate one another and play power games. When I mentioned my topic, people usually assumed that the focus would be on the failures of friendship, whereas my own interest was in successful friendship: how does it work when it does work? Surely these reactions reveal something of friendship's particular difficulty in our culture, but one element of that difficulty is the knee-jerk terror of sentimentality. Perhaps it protects us from commitments that we feel unable to make.

"As a writer," says John Irving, "it is cowardly to so fear sentimentality that one avoids it altogether. . . . A fear of contamination by soap opera haunts the educated writer—and the reader. . . . And when we writers—in our own work—escape the slur of sentimentality, we should ask ourselves if what we are doing matters" (3, 96).

Whatever the cause, our failure to take on the matter of friendship has impoverished our relationships as deeply as it has our discourse. For our language of friendship and our conceptions of it affect the way in which we actually experience friendship: our expectations, our hopes, our fears, our satisfactions, and our disappointments. It seems clear that friendship has been relegated to the cultural attic as much out of fear of sentimentality as out of a sense that it can easily be explained away as self-interested. This book takes a humbler stance before the complexities and mysteries of friendship than that of the cynic, and a more tough-minded view than that of the sentimentalist. In so doing it attempts to bring friendship downstairs again: to recover the tradition and put the subject back on the cultural agenda.

Though I make no attempt to be exhaustive in my treatment of the literature, I do deal with many of the major writers and works in this tradition: Aristotle, Cicero, Shakespeare, Montaigne, Johnson, Austen, Thoreau, Gaskell, Nietzsche, Whitman, Hemingway, Auden, Hellman, and Rich, among others. Everyone will have his list of unforgivable omissions. My own extends to many pages and begins with Plato, whose *Lysis* is devoted exclusively to friendship and whose *Symposium, Republic, Laws,* and *Phaedrus* also touch on it. But the enigmatic *Lysis* notwithstanding, friendship is more the environment or ethos than the subject of Plato's dialogues. It is the presiding spirit of Socrates's whole philosophical enterprise but, in contrast with Aristotle's treatment of the subject, it rarely is discussed directly. In any case, though my discussions of literary works will, I hope, be useful as ends in themselves, they are also intended as examples, as points of departure, or as ways of illuminating particular points in my general argument about friendship.

When I first began thinking about this book, I shared some of my early conceptions and plans with Kenneth Burke, who, well into his eighties now, continues to be one of our most ambitious and wide-ranging literary critics and theorists. "That's a good project you have lined up," he told me. "You are henceforth to be under the threat of gridlock." Gridlock is what happened to traffic in New York City during the subway strike a few years ago. Cars converged from so many directions at once that no one could move, and that, of course, is what he was warning me about: friendship is such a broad subject and it can be approached from so many different directions—each of which has important implications for every other—that the big danger in undertaking this kind of a study is simple paralysis.

Add to this problem the fact that the subject has been neglected for years, and it should be obvious that no single book can pretend to cover the entire field. One could write a history of friendship, a sociology and an anthropology of friendship, an ethics, a cross-cultural study, a discussion of friendship from the point of view of politics or developmental psychology, or simply an old-fashioned anatomy of friendship. One could examine the friendship of soldiers at war, of teachers and students, husbands and wives, fellow workers, business partners, children, adolescents, adults, and the elderly. When I first began my study of friendship, I thought that this book would provide something like a comprehensive picture of friendship in our culture, systematically exploring such issues as the influence on friendship of developments within the family, within the institution of marriage, within the workplace, in sexual relations, in patterns of mobility and social structure. I would explore current assumptions about personal identity and the self; I would study the secularization of the ideal of brotherly love and various other religious legacies; I would consider the impact of capitalism on friendship, of democracy and a wide range of other social, political, and economic matters. I did, in fact, write two more chapters that explore just such issues, but I have, for the present, put them aside. For it has become increasingly apparent to me that even a half-dozen new books on friendship would barely scratch the surface of this immense—and immensely fascinating—topic.

It will also quickly become apparent that I begin with no particular definition of friendship. Dr. Johnson's quip about poetry seems to me the better part of wisdom about friendship as well: "What is poetry?" Boswell asks him in his *Life*. "Why, sir," Johnson replies, "it is much easier to say what it is not. We all *know* what light is; but it is not easy to *tell* what it is" (744). What interests me is the extraordinary variety of friendship's forms, not only across historical periods and cultures but even within a given culture. This book, however, is not about everything related to friendship or the spirit of friendliness. The emphasis is rather on close, usually nonsexual relationships of mutual regard and affection between people who are not kin. I organize my material under two large conceptions: form and gift. The first chapter, "Friendship and Form," deals with the problems that arise in a culture like ours, where our democratic aversion to ceremony, our puritanical suspicion of ritual, and our romantic ideology of authenticity make us try to circumvent or explode forms in personal relationships. I argue that form functions in friendship, as it does in art, as something that promotes rather than obstructs intimacy, and I examine the numerous ways that we generate and create form and ritual in our relationships when none are socially prescribed, as they are in most other societies.

The second chapter, "Friendship as Gift Exchange," draws on the recent work of Lewis Hyde. Though he does not discuss friendship, Hyde's theory of the gift has crucial implications for our understanding of friendship, especially for the spiritual dimensions of that relationship. In my final chapter I examine the treatment of the issues I have been discussing—friendship, form, and gift exchange—in one major literary work: *The Merchant of Venice*. I use this play because it is widely known and because it deals as directly and profoundly with the questions I address throughout the book as any work I know.

It may be useful, then, in undertaking a reevaluation of friendship, to recognize the persistence of form and gift in the literature and to understand their continuing vitality as metaphors for friendship. To underline their importance I have purposely limited my focus to those two broad issues. My modest hope for this book is that its sketches will inspire fuller and more detailed canvases, and that some of those sketches will be valuable in themselves.

1 Friendship and Form

"Nothing is more pitiful than the arrogant disdain of most of our contemporaries for questions of form, for the smallest questions of form have acquired in our time an importance which they never had before; many of the greatest interests of mankind depend upon them."—Alexis de Tocqueville, *Democracy in America*

The anthropologist Robert Brain tells us that in Mali

> best friends throw excrement at each other and comment loudly on the genitals of their respective parents—this, to us, unnatural and obscene behaviour is a proof of the love of friends. . . . In Tanzania, if a man meets a woman who is his special friend, he may insult her, throw her to the ground, and pummel her like a boxing bag. In New Guinea, when a man acquires a trading partner he "falls in love" with him as part of the deal. . . . In southern Ghana, friends who love each other marry, the "husband" paying bridewealth to his friend's parents. In Latin America, a friendly tie between two men may be enhanced by performing a Christian rite of baptism over a tree—both men in this way become devoted godsibs (co-godparents or gossips) of the christened tree. (10)[1]

These ethnographic examples seem strange to us not simply because they are exotic, but because they picture friendship as a highly formal and ritualized activity, just the opposite of our own popular conception. Most modern Americans assume that ceremony and artifice obstruct rather than facilitate intimacy, especially in that most unstructured of relationships, friendship. Forgoing the security of knowing explicitly the duties and expectations of friendships, we tend to value such relationships precisely because they are not formalized and legalized. Unlike many other cultures, ours has provided scarcely any institutional framework or formal patterning for friendship. For Americans, it would appear, friendship and form are utterly alien to each other.

The reasons for this state of affairs are complex, but clearly they have something to do with our general suspicion of form in America. The two deepest currents here are the religious and the political-economic. On the one hand we have the puritanical suspicion of ritual, and on the other, the democratic aversion to ceremony. Both associate ritual with a tyrannical and hierarchical agent; in one case the established church, and in the other, aristocracy. Without exploring these influences further, it seems safe to assert that in its very foundations American culture has within it a profound skepticism about form, and a readiness to associate it with whatever constricts freedom and obstructs equality.

Over a century ago de Tocqueville observed that "men living in democratic ages do not readily comprehend the utility of forms: they feel an instinctive contempt for them . . . as they commonly aspire to easy and present gratifications, they rush onwards to the object of their desire, and the slightest delay exasperates them" (344).[2] Any complete account of Americans' anxiety about form in friendship would have to take account of our traditional ideals of individualism and freedom of choice, and of our fascination with spontaneity and change, for surely these contribute significantly to a cultural context inimical to the establishment of ceremony in friendship. But I should like to suggest that friendship cannot flourish at all outside of forms.

Without affection, it is obvious that no amount of ritual

can make a friendship survive. But I would argue that, far from obstructing intimacy, form promotes and enables it—in friendship as in all human relationships. The question is not whether we ought to formalize and ritualize our friendships, but how we already do so, despite our culture's ideological anxiety about ceremony and its paucity of institutions for preserving friendship. In a culture like ours, where there are relatively few socially prescribed forms for friendship, we have two choices. We can either attempt to circumvent forms altogether in our relationships or we can master what forms remain and invent new ones.[3] Overwhelmingly, in recent years, our tendency has been to try to circumvent, even to explode forms—so much so that the opposition to form has become a fascinating ideology in its own right. In the realm of friendship its consequences have, I shall argue, been frustrating at best and destructive at worst. For friendship and form are *not* antagonistic, a point that will become especially evident when we discover the extent to which much behavior that seems informal, even antiformal, can more accurately be seen as simply formal in a different way.

If mastering residual forms and inventing new ones is preferable to trying to ignore or explode forms altogether, it still cannot be seen as a fully adequate substitute for more public social institutions and cultural forms. Perhaps the biggest price we pay for this privatization of friendship is that there is now a great deal of uncertainty surrounding the expectations and duties of friendship. But there is also a much greater opportunity for creativity. In our culture, says Brain, friends "are left to find their own symbols and make up their own rituals—private jokes, special greetings, nicknames, regular meetings" (106). In order to demonstrate some of the ways in which form functions in friendship, I want to examine some of those rituals, both through literary examples and through illustrations drawn from our daily lives. For those rituals are often of a density, complexity, and beauty that warrants our considering them on analogy with works of art and other imaginative constructs that both create and interpret realities. In the playground of friendship, within clear boundaries of trust and affection, and not-so-clear boundaries of vulnerability and risk, friends invent and play the most serious games. These games explore, hypothesize, interpret, test, and validate their players' experiences, identities, and values; and if we are to understand them, we must first of all see them as formal constructs and put aside the naive popular notion that in matters of intimacy all forms are suspect.

In childhood, rituals are very much in the foreground. One thinks of the rings or half-moon necklaces that are still exchanged by girls as tokens of friendship; or the solemn discussions (in one instance I can remember, a nearly Talmudic disputation) about whether one ought to be "best friends" with Bobby or Joe—and then the formal declarations to one's classmates. Iona and Peter Opie have documented the ritual chants, the jingles and ceremonies that British schoolchildren continue to perform for the making and breaking of friendships. The words "Make friends, make friends, / Never, never break friends" have been chanted by millions of British children who often link little fingers moistened with saliva in the process (324). And I have a distant memory of the first time I raided my mother's sewing box for a needle with which to prick my own and my friend's fingers so that we could truly become blood brothers.

In adolescence and young adulthood, rituals in friendship can be observed most easily on playing fields and in fraternity and sorority houses. We generally acknowledge dating and courting as ritual activities, but we have been less inclined to view the courting of friends in this way, for youngsters and adults alike. The second or third dinner invitation has come to assume that status for many couples. The invitation to lunch, to have a drink, to go to the football game—the invitation itself functions for us in a tacit but carefully regulated way, whose nuances of timing, repetition, and a hundred other factors must be understood by both parties if the complicated transaction of sentiment that it represents is to succeed. There is a wonderful moment in Fred Uhlman's *Reunion* when the adolescent Jewish hero, Hans, courts the friendship of his German classmate Konradin. "All I knew, then, was that he was going to be my friend," says Hans. "The problem was how to attract him to me." Hans shows off for Konradin in class, discussing *Madame Bovary* and Homer, attacking Schiller and calling Heine "a poet for commercial travellers." In gym class, he volunteers to perform on the horizontal bar. "I had no fear," he says, "only one will and one desire. I was going to do it for *him*." Hemingway describes the young bullfighter Pedro Romero in a similar way as he courts Brett in *The Sun Also Rises,* but Uhlman rescues the scene from bathos—and from the cynical suspicion of homosexuality—in the next comic sentence: "Suddenly I raised my body right up, jumped over the bar, flew in the air—and then thump!" (26, 28, 31)

Later in this novella, which is set in Germany in the thirties and portrays a passionate adolescent friendship doomed when Konradin admits his sympathy for Hitler, Hans visits Konradin's home for the first time:

> [Konradin] rushed to a cupboard and with an eagerness which showed me how long he had been waiting for this occasion, his eyes shining in anticipation of my envy and wonder, he laid out his treasures. Out of their cotton wool he took his Greek coins. . . . But this wasn't all; other treasures followed, more precious than any of mine: a goddess from Gela in Sicily, a small bottle from Cyprus the colour and shape of an orange with geometrical designs on it . . . a Roman vase the colour of milky pale-green jade and a small Greek bronze figure of Hercules. It was touching to see his delight at being able to show me this collection and to watch my amazement and my admiration. (76–77)

Collections are very important for children and adolescents; their mystique is tied up with the child's sense of himself and of his connection with the world. My older son, who is nine, has seashells, pinecones, miniature animals, and rocks in his collection, but also his first scorecard from miniature golf, a tiny paper umbrella that punctured his cousin's maraschino cherry at dessert last summer at the beach, the stuffed toy alligator that my father received as a gag gift when he was in the hospital, and a dozen other disparate items that represent important events and experiences for him in his encounter with the world beyond his home. To share one's collection is to share something of both one's inner world and one's imaginative gatherings-in of the outer world. Adults share collections as well—not usually of material things but of experience. One of the crucial stages in the formation of most friendships is the long conversation in which one shares one's past with one's emerging friend, in which one displays what one has done, what one has collected by way of experience, and offers it up for the friend's examination. The gesture itself grants to the friend a kind of ritualistic admission to one's interior room, a symbolic invitation to cross over the border between one's public and private selves. As with children, it is not only what one presents that affects the friendship but also how it is presented.

We might consider this formulation in its broadest application as a description of the fundamental exchange that friendship involves. What one presents in a friendship is not simply one's "self" (a slippery-enough concept that we will have more to say about later) but also one's sense of the world. As with art, the form and content of one's "presentation" stand in a complex dialectical relationship with each other, and with the parallel dialectic of one's friend's presentation. What each party presents and how he presents it will define the friendship.

Two classics among the set pieces of friendship are the parting of friends and the meal that celebrates their reunion. I want to compare two of Pound's translations from the Chinese of *Li T'ai Po* with two modern novels that treat these stock situations in different ways. "Taking Leave of a Friend" is short enough to quote completely:

> Blue mountains to the north of the walls,
> White river winding about them;
> Here we must make separation
> And go out through a thousand miles of dead grass.
> Wind like a floating wide cloud,
> Sunset like the parting of old acquaintances

> Who bow over their clasped hands at a distance.
> Our horses neigh to each other
> > as we are departing.

(137)

The horses neighing to each other provide a parallel in the natural world to the cultural act of bowing "over their clasped hands"—a gesture that is ceremonial enough in itself to make it seem inappropriately distant to us, to say nothing of the fact that the "old acquaintances" do so literally "at a distance." Compare this parting to Hemingway's description of the parting of Mike, Bill, and Jake toward the end of *The Sun Also Rises:*

> At the hotel where Mike was going to stay in Saint Jean we stopped the car and he got out. The chauffeur carried in his bags. Mike stood by the side of the car.
> "Good-bye, you chaps," Mike said. "It was a damned fine fiesta."
> "So long, Mike," Bill said.
> "I'll see you around," I said.
> "Don't worry about money," Mike said. "You can pay for the car, Jake, and I'll send you my share."
> "So long, Mike."
> "So long, you chaps. You've been damned nice."
> We all shook hands. We waved from the car to Mike. He stood in the road watching. We got to Bayonne just before the train left. A porter carried Bill's bags in from the consigne. I went as far as the inner gate to the tracks.
> "So long, fella," Bill said.
> "So long, kid!"
> "It was swell. I've had a swell time."
> "Will you be in Paris?"
> "No, I have to sail on the 17th. So long, fella!"
> "So long, old kid!"
> He went in through the gate to the train. The porter went ahead with the bags. I watched the train pull out. Bill was at one of the windows. The window passed, the rest of the train passed, and the tracks were empty. I went outside to the car. (231)

The forms are different here but they are as rigidly prescribed as the bowing. The handshakes, the waving, the clipped expressions of thanks and enjoyment, the recourse to words like "chaps," "fella," and "old kid"—all of these are ways of expressing affection in a culture that denies men more physical expressions. When Jake says to Bill, "So long, old kid!", he is saying goodbye to a friend in as formal and conventional a way as an eighteenth-century English poet writing heroic couplets—or a late twentieth-century American college student writing free verse. The bow of those Chinese friends may seem overly formal to us, but actually it is only formal in a different way. Jake would no more bow to Bill than he would hug him—but modern American women in a similar situation would have hugged quite naturally.[4]

In Pound's translation of "Exile's Letter," So-Kiu of Rakuyo invites his old friend, whom he has not seen for a long time and who lives far away, to visit him:

> And what with broken wheels and so on, I won't say it wasn't hard going,
> Over roads twisted like sheep's guts.
> And I was still going, late in the year,
>   in the cutting wind from the North,
> And thinking how little you cared for the cost,
>   and you caring enough to pay it.
> And what a reception:
> Red jade cups, food well set on a blue jewelled table,
> And I was drunk, and had no thought of returning.
> And you would walk out with me to the western corner of the castle,
> To the dynastic temple, with water about it clear as blue jade,
> With boats floating, and the sound of mouth-organs and drums,
> With ripples like dragon-scales, going grass green on the water,
> Pleasure lasting, with courtezans, going and coming without hindrance,
> With the willow flakes falling like snow,

And the vermilioned girls getting drunk about sunset,
And the water, a hundred feet deep, reflecting green eyebrows
—Eyebrows painted green are a fine sight in young moonlight,
Gracefully painted—
And the girls singing back at each other,
Dancing in transparent brocade,
And the wind lifting the song, and interrupting it,
Tossing it up under the clouds.
And all this comes to an end.
And is not again to be met with.

Many people today feel no need to be fancy with an old friend, even if they have not seen him for a long time. If he were coming to visit they would probably try to keep the evening casual. They might, for example, eat on the everyday dishes in the kitchen. Others would eat on paper plates on the porch and spend the evening trying to confirm their ideology that there is no need to be formal among friends. Nor would they notice just how formalized and conventionalized their so-called informality has become in recent years. But others would bring out the china and eat on a tablecloth in the dining room even if they don't have "red jade cups" and a "blue jewelled table." And they might do so even if they were on very familiar terms with their friend, because at some level they recognize that a formal meal still has considerable ritual power. The emotional, even the spiritual, difference between Thanksgiving or Christmas dinner and a regular meal is clear enough, but the successful reunion dinner with a friend is just as ritualistically charged as the holiday meal. It provides a kind of arena for the reentry or reemergence of one's friendship. A bountiful table, the passing and sharing of good food, even the skill and labor of preparing a table and a meal are all tied up, symbolically, with the spirit of generosity, nurture, liberality, and cheerfulness that is being rekindled in the friendship and, as it were, ritualistically celebrated at the feast.[5] They also help establish a kind of neutral zone in which everyone can engage in an external—and pleasant—activity that spares everyone the awkwardness of trying to talk intimately too soon after the reunion. Especially during the period when friends are becoming reacquainted after separation, the rules and forms of hospitality provide a clearly comprehensible language in which they can express their good will and friendliness without what at this stage might be the awkwardness of direct verbal expression of friendship.

The most frequent sound at reunion dinner tables is laughter, partly the awkward kind that allows friends to readjust and reorient themselves to their old friends. In Philip Schultz's forthcoming novel, *Upstart Crows,* the two central characters, who met and became best of friends in graduate school, have been separated for quite a while. No sooner does Max show up unexpectedly on Raphael's doorstep than they are sitting down to an elaborate meal—and laughing! "Now it's my notion," says Raph, "that we don't laugh so much at what is said, at any intellectual connecting of images, but at the good feeling, the mirth, the building up of humor in someone's chest; a psychic calling!" (61). What builds up, I would suggest, is the spirit of the friendship itself, and it is that spirit that provides the good feeling and leads to both the laughter and the urge to have a meal, each of which is a kind of celebration.

The backdrop to all this mirth is separation. "And all this comes to an end," says Pound's Chinese poet. "And is not again to be met with." The great feasts of Homeric epic and the magnificent drinking parties in the mead halls of *Beowulf* share with Pound's and Schultz's celebrations an affirmation of friendship and camaraderie despite the ravages of time. That same affirmation in the teeth of death can be seen in that other highly formalized ritual of friendship, the Irish wake. And Keats, perhaps the supreme poet of transitory joys, fills his work with ritual meals, and refers in his letters to "the wine of love—and the Bread of Friendship" (1.283).

The sacramental quality with which Keats endows daily life survives in innumerable corners of our lives in addition to dinner parties for old friends. To identify it we need to look for modern analogues to the old forms. The scene that

Pound gives us in "Exile's Letter," for example, is as artificial as one could imagine. Those "vermilioned girls" have "eyebrows painted green," which "are a fine sight in young moonlight, / Gracefully painted," and the girls are "singing back at each other" in a gesture as formal as their "dancing in transparent brocade." Nietzsche says that since we are not gods, we should not aspire to nakedness with our friends: "For thy friend," he says, "thou canst not adorn thyself beautifully enough" (*Zarathustra* 74). Like Pound, Nietzsche suggests that forms are a mark of—not an impediment to—our humanity. We live in the artifices we create and we reveal ourselves to our friends not by trying to strip away our clothes but by wearing them artfully. Formality, ritual, hospitality, artifice—these do not hinder intimacy; they enhance it.

No one has embodied that insight with such exquisite relish and calm poetic confidence as W. H. Auden, whose *About the House* celebrates the innumerable ways in which daily life is spiritually transfigured precisely by means of form.

In "Tonight at Seven-Thirty," for example, Auden sings a comic but tender hymn praising—of all things—the institution of the dinner party. Unlike plants, whose life "is one continuous solitary meal," and unlike "ruminants," "predators," and "pack-hunters,"

> Only man,
> supererogatory beast,
> Dame Kind's thoroughbred lunatic, can
> do the honors of a feast.

Hospitality's position is privileged:

> The right of a guest
> to standing and foster is as old
> as the ban on incest.

Auden proceeds to outline rather fastidious standards for the ideal dinner party:

> a dinner party,
> however select,

is a worldly rite that nicknames or endearments
> or family
diminutives would profane: two doters who wish
to tiddle and curmurr between the soup and fish
belong in restaurants, all children should be fed
> earlier and be safely in bed.
Well-liking, though, is a must.

Demanding as his standards of admission are, Auden wants no gods at his party, for they "would be too odd/to talk to and, despite . . . imposing presence, a bore." What he wants is

> men
and women who enjoy the cloop of corks, appreciate
> depatical fare, yet can see in swallowing
> > a sign of reverence,
> in speech a work of re-presenting
> > the true olamic silence.

One room in Auden's house is set aside, as the title of another of his poems in this volume suggests, "For Friends Only." That guest room is "a shrine to friendship . . . in a house backed by orderly woods." The note again is formality, but the kind that promotes, rather than inhibits, freedom:

> Books we do have for almost any
> Literate mood, and notepaper, envelopes,
> For a writing one (to "borrow" stamps
> Is a mark of ill-breeding):
> Between lunch and tea, perhaps a drive;
> After dinner, music or gossip.

Opportunities for intimate talk are available, not obligatory:

> Should you have troubles (pets will die,
> Lovers are always behaving badly)
> And compassion helps, we will hear it,
> Examine and give our counsel:
> If to mention them hurts too much,
> We shall not be nosey.

The tone here reveals genuine tenderness aligned with the kind of tact that saves compassion from becoming an ideology. After all, Auden says:

> Easy at first, the language of friendship
> Is, as we soon discover,
> Very difficult to speak well, a tongue
> With no cognates, no resemblance
> To the galimatias of nursery and bedroom,
> Court rhyme or shepherd's prose,
>
> And, unless often spoken, soon goes rusty.
> Distance and duties divide us,
> But absence will not seem an evil
> If it make our re-meeting
> A real occasion. Come when you can:
> Your room will be ready.

That "distance and duties divide" friends may not be an exclusively modern phenomenon, but it certainly is characteristically modern. Auden not only accepts that reality; he finds in it a grain of good fortune, because absence makes reunions even sweeter. In the language, syntax, and rhythm of those final lines, which so brilliantly combine the formal and the intimate, Auden's house of form clearly becomes a home.

If friendship requires a sensitivity to form, its fundamental problem today is that form and artifice have acquired a bad reputation. Part of that reputation, as I suggested earlier, is a function of our puritan heritage, with its aversion to ritual, and of the tendency of the egalitarian spirit to associate ceremony with class structure. I also suggested earlier that we place such a high premium on change and freedom of choice that we are reluctant to commit ourselves to relationships that bring with them explicit requirements and obligations over time. Santayana, for example, fears destroying friendship by turning it into "an odious obligation. . . . It is essential to friendship to be free," he says, "and to assume no liability in matters below its liberal sphere" (84). One can share his anxiety over swearing eternal friendship and one can also share his concern about turning what should be a relationship of giving into one of obligation.[6] My whole next chapter, in fact, is devoted to the importance for friendship of precisely that distinction. But Santayana's assumptions about freedom seem naive, for surely there are situations in which one voluntarily relinquishes some freedom and accepts certain rules precisely in order to gain a higher freedom. That, I take it, is what happens in the best of friendships, as it does in the best of marriages. This is, as we shall see, a central theme of *The Merchant of Venice*. And is it not one crucial function of form in the arts? The question is not whether form is being used, but whether it is being used creatively. After all, forms change, and they interact subtly with other social forms. If form is not being used creatively, it can of course be rigid and stultifying; likewise, there is always the danger of overformalizing a relationship so that it becomes arid or grotesque. But these cases do not argue against form; they merely reveal its fallibility. For whatever its difficulties, form remains creativity's truest mode of freedom—in the arts and in personal relationships alike. We need to be mindful of the dangers, but today we ought to be much more concerned with the opposite threat, namely, that we impoverish our friendships by denying them ceremonial patterning. "Why should we insist," asks Brain, "that love stand on its own two feet in the case of friends, when two romantic lovers who also love each other with all their heart and soul, until death do them part, hedge in their passion with a wedding ceremony, oaths, and legal contracts? In denying friendship formal bonds our society seems to undervalue love, not value it" (18). Later, Brain asks, "Are we afraid that a formalization and ritualization of friendship roles would make them as unambiguous and permanent as those between husband and wife—and therefore inescapable?" (105).

Brain is referring here to the fact that we have few social institutions for friendship in our culture, and that is surely one reflection of our suspicion of "formal bonds," as he calls them. But the problem of form goes far beyond institutions in our culture—and far beyond our puritan and democratic heritage. It is as much a private as a public problem, and in the realm of the private it is complicated and distorted terribly by our pervasive ethic of authenticity.

Lionel Trilling's brilliant analysis in *Sincerity and Authenticity* brings the complex issues of its title into focus in a way that I can scarcely hint at here. But what he says is much to our point. The ethic of authenticity, according to Trilling, proposes being true to oneself not as a means to some other end (such as avoiding falsehood to others) but as an end in itself. "At the behest of the criterion of authenticity, much that was once thought to make up the very fabric of culture has come to seem of little account, mere fantasy or ritual, or downright falsification" (11). The movement is clear: ritual comes to be considered "mere" ritual, i.e., empty, false, or mechanical, and "it was the mechanical principle," says Trilling, "which was felt to be the enemy of being, the source of inauthenticity" (127). Increasingly, we come to regard form as an impediment to authenticity, particularly in personal relationships.

In recent years the ideal of authenticity has become something of a popular ideology, whose emergence in the popular culture can be seen in the popularity of a book like *The Catcher in the Rye* (with its obsessive fear of the "phony") during the early sixties and, more triumphantly, in the flourishing of the encounter group movement later in that decade. Some of those groups have a clear and laudable therapeutic function but many of them are based on an ideology of authenticity that pitifully reifies—and thus distorts—the whole notion of a "relationship." Beginning with the assumption that relationships "fulfill needs," and are therefore "meaningful," this ideology allows one to purchase the idea of friendship without soiling one's hands, for in fact the emphasis is on discovering *oneself,* not another, and on gratifying *oneself,* not another. The object is to make contact with one's own deepest—i.e., most authentic—self. In many of these groups, to suggest a turn on the revealing California jokes, one cannot only have a friend, one can "experience" friendship.[7]

I hesitate to attack such a vulnerable target, but I believe the institutionalization of encounter groups is a significant development in the history of friendship. Perhaps even more than computer dating services, encounter groups depend on a loneliness that is as pervasive as the decline of friendship. Most of us know people who have been helped by these groups, but we also know people whose central reason for attending is that they have no other friends. Not only do we find more people treating friendship as a therapeutic relationship; we also find more people turning to therapy because they cannot make friends. Pop psychology and sociology love a vacuum.

Authenticity in friendship is so rare and admirable that it would be ridiculous to exaggerate its limitations. The ideal of authenticity is not inevitably damaging to friendship, but it can be when it makes an ideology of the self. "At a certain point in history," Trilling says, "men became individuals." Until then, man did not "imagine himself . . . standing outside or above his own personality." The word *self* began to be used "not as a mere reflexive or intensive, but as an autonomous noun referring, the *O.E.D.* tells us, to 'that . . . in a person [which] is really and intrinsically *he* (in contradistinction to what is adventitious)'" (24–25). On this model, friends could get closer only by peeling away the supposedly artificial layers of their selves until they got to some presumably naked core, the authentic self. But what if, as Nietzsche and Pound suggest, those "artificial" layers actually constitute, rather than disguise, the self? And what if they constitute it in the way that the layers of an onion constitute the onion? Peel them away and you will find exposed not a central kernel but thin air. The self, as Blake said, is not a genie in a bottle.

The problem of the self has been the subject of some of the most serious philosophical investigation of the last two centuries. I do not mean to speak glibly of its numerous perplexities. After all, if there is no core or essential self, to what is it that one relates in a friendship? I shall return to this and related questions later, but for now I simply want to suggest that the issue of sincerity and authenticity is inextricably involved with one's sense of the self, and that the dynamics of that conceptual complex bear directly on friendship.

The ideal of authenticity may impose strict demands on a

friendship, not least because of its skepticism about form, but no one can deny the importance of this ideal in another sense. Perhaps the single most pervasive theme in the literature of friendship is the need for sincerity and openness. "There can be no element of show or pretense," says Cicero; "there can be no element of deception or hypocrisy" (58). Sincerity demands that there be no gap between (to use Trilling's terms) "avowal and actual feeling" (2); consequently, the greatest danger to friendship, according to Cicero, is "servility, sycophancy and flattery," all of which measure things by what people want to hear rather than by the truth (85). "No," says Hamlet,

> let the candied tongue lick absurd pomp,
> And crook the pregnant hinges of the knee
> Where thrift may follow fawning.
> (3.2.60–62)

Hamlet will have no part of such hypocrisy, and he cherishes Horatio—in contrast to the conniving Rosencrantz and Guildenstern, who "think I am easier to be played on than a pipe" (3.2.360–61)—partly because Horatio is sincere.

Sincerity in this sense is of course crucial to friendship. Duplicity, deception, prevarication are fatal. But having acknowledged that obvious point, it is incumbent on us to recognize that, contrary to current assumptions, direct communication is not always—I would say not usually—the best way to honor the ethic of sincerity or authenticity. Intimacy may come out of direct expression, but it is scarcely guaranteed and it certainly can be produced in other ways as well. There are, to be sure, times when friends must and should talk with utter frankness and abandon. The stereotypical version of this encounter can be seen on any soap opera when, at two in the afternoon, the housewife hears a knock at her door, opens it, and finds a friend in distress. "Janet, please. I need to talk." Steaming coffee, a roaring fire, some true confession, and for a moment the pain is bearable.

Television is an even easier target than encounter groups, but the model of intimacy it presents is only a more sentimentalized version of our dominant American model. Both assume that the self is what remains when all the layers have been peeled away and that friends can make contact with that inner core only by thus peeling back the layers. This model assumes that, to the extent that it is both necessary and important for friends to be open with each other, they must do so by removing formal obstacles to their intimacy and approaching it head-on. The idea is that we get close by circumventing or exploding forms, not following them. One even sees this principle in the weatherman on the eleven o'clock news who talks to his thousands of viewers as though they were all buddies. By the very act of trying to make an impersonal situation personal, he ends up sounding even more artificial than the weatherman who follows the conventions of formality because he recognizes that broadcasting the weather on television is not the same thing as chatting about the weather with friends in a living room. Or consider the man who recently called "to wish you happy birthday, Ron." "Thanks," I said, trying to figure out who he was. "So how things goin' for ya, kid?" he asked, with that by now readily detectable rehearsed familiarity. Never having met or spoken to this person, who now identified himself as "ole Gary Harrison" from an insurance company, I felt embarrassed, but he pressed on with the kind of casual chitchat someone in his sales seminar told him friends engage in. After a few minutes, he told me he had no business—"Just calling to say hi"—and asked me if it wasn't nice to get a social call once in a while instead of a business call. For the weatherman pretending to chat casually about the weather with a friend, and for the insurance salesman posturing as my old buddy, wishing away the conventions does not make them vanish; here, as in other situations, it throws them into relief.

Consider an analogous situation in literature. The sonnet, which on first view would seem too narrow and constricting for the expression of intimacy, has been our most successful form for love poetry. Or consider the studiously embellished conceits and structures of a poem like Donne's "A Valediction: Forbidding Mourning," which is among the most tender love poems in the language. The contrary impulse, the attempt to break through the mask, is usually doomed, even in contemporary confessional poetry, whose strategies of defying convention have themselves become highly conventional. Likewise, I would suggest, the frank conversation with a friend cannot, in our time, escape the conventions of sincerity and authenticity. Our experience of such a conversation, and our expectations of intimacy, will be shaped by those conventions as surely as our writing (or reading) of a confessional poem will be shaped by the already elaborate conventions of confessional poetry. The confessional mode continues to be popular—in friendship as in the arts. But as any psychiatrist or autobiographer knows, cutting through to some presumably fundamental truth about oneself is always a task of extraordinary difficulty. That the attempt has become so popular in our time only complicates the matter and may well, ironically, make it more rather than less difficult. Like its older cousin Sentimentality and its younger cousins Studied Casualness and Earnest Informality, Confession has become a very difficult form to use creatively, which is why it fails in friendship as often as it does in poetry.

There are times, as well, when openness is simply tactless and can end up being cruel. In *Reunion,* Hans is terribly embarrassed by the first meeting of his father and Konradin:

> I trembled violently and could hardly keep back my tears. I had only one wish: never to see Konradin again. But he, who must have understood what was going on in my mind, seemed to be busy looking at my books. If he hadn't done so, if at this moment he had talked to me, worse still if he had tried to console me, to touch me, I should have hit him. . . . But he instinctively did the right thing. He gave me time to recover and when after five minutes he turned round and smiled at me I could smile back between my tears. (69–70)

We call this the "art" of friendship, and in this light the cliché takes on fresh meaning, though its wisdom has been the subject of many a quip. "When my friends are one-eyed," says Joubert, "I look at their profile" (qtd. in B. Stevenson 739). "To find a friend," says Norman Douglas, "one must close one eye—to keep him, two" (qtd. in Peter 215). The cynical inversion of this principle is put beautifully by Pascal: "I lay it down as a fact that, if all men knew what others say of them, there would not be four friends in the world" (qtd. in B. Stevenson 727).

Apparently we are not designed to take too much sincerity. "It is necessary," says Plutarch, "to treat frankness as a fine art . . . always needing . . . a tempering with moderation" ("Flatterer" 393; cf. 351, 365). Though tact may often be the gentler course, there are other, more subtle games we invent in order to relate intimately without recourse to the direct assault. At the risk of considerable personal awkwardness, let me recount one of these from my own experience.

My best friend and I have enjoyed an extraordinary relationship since we were seven years old. As we were growing up, we used the word *big* to characterize our heroes, who were mainly baseball and football players. By the time we reached high school one of our friends, a first baseman, was being scouted by major league teams. He was big, we realized, but just how big? Would he make the majors? Would he actually play one Saturday afternoon in Cleveland Municipal Stadium? Would he be an All-Star? World Series? Hall of Fame? Best ever?

We had no idea of the continuity with which we used this simple but potent word *big,* but years later I could see a fascinating pattern. For I realized that we had used exactly the same word to deal with our new set of aspirations after we had gone off to college and abandoned our fantasies about being—or being friends with—professional athletes. During our first Thanksgiving vacation together, having returned from our separate colleges, my friend and I bragged to each other about our professors.

"My philosophy and biology profs have Ph.D.s," he said, "and my other two are just finishing their dissertations."

"Means nothing," I countered; "all these guys have doctorates. What matters is where they're from. My Spanish teacher did hers at Oxford."

"Oxford?" he said, half incredulously. "That's even bigger than Harvard or Yale."

But next year at this time, two of his professors were from Oxford so the issue now was not schools but reputations.

"This guy's unreal," he said. "One of the two or three biggest guys in political science in the country."

"Not the *world?*" I mocked—only because I had nothing to top him. Nothing, that is, until spring vacation of our junior year, when I reported that I had studied in Madrid with the niece of Spain's greatest scholar and that I had actually met this man and talked with him about literature. "This guy isn't big, I mean he's . . . what can I say? He's gigantic, monumental!"

We went on in this ridiculous vein for a few years, moving up a hierarchy of doctorate/affiliation/reputation which, in our minds, was utterly straightforward, though we hadn't an inkling that it was a mere transposition of the major league/All-Star/Hall of Fame hierarchy that we had recently abandoned. The apparent crassness of our concern with success can be seen in a gentler light when one realizes that neither of us had grown up in the world of art and ideas. Books, concerts, museums were for the most part alien to us. Not until our last year of high school did we discover that world, and it seemed to us as foreign as it was fascinating. The energy that before had gone exclusively to sports and social life we now channeled in this strange new direction, without the slightest sense of what actually went on in that world or how one actually moved in it.

It was not long before we began to open up an ironic perspective on our naive yearning and youthful ambition. As our graduate school professors began to urge us to publish this or that paper, we exchanged long distance phone calls that often began with a booming, bumptious claim of "I'm big! Oh, am I big!" This would be followed by histrionically sober questioning by the other party (no humor was allowed at this point because you had to let the other guy tell you his good news), and then raucous laughter that nervously released any envy on one side or embarrassment on the other, and—these are not in contradiction—expressed our mutual joy in the success of one of us.

One day, when we were teaching at the same college in different departments, my friend and I spent an hysterical hour making pencil marks on a wall in his office to establish exactly where we and our teachers and colleagues would stand in relation to the likes of Plato, Shakespeare, and Tocqueville. We were fully conscious at that point of the primitive absurdity of our conception of "big," but I do not think we were aware that we had used it so often in the past, and of course we did not know that we would be using it again—for very serious purposes—in the future.

Though this friendship has been proceeding intensely for over thirty years, for more than half of that time it has taken place largely through long distance calls. My friend and I have seen each other frequently, but except for a two-year period, we have lived in different places since graduating from high school. Aristotle tells us that "nothing characterizes friends as much as living in each other's company," and that if you extend friendship but do not actually live together, you really do not have friendship so much as good will, which is prerequisite to friendship but different from it (223, 255). It is difficult to exaggerate the importance for friendship of the frequency with which we move from town to town. "The proportion of friends most people attempt to keep in touch with after a move is small," says Graham Allen, a sociologist who has studied this situation in considerable detail. "Even with these there is difficulty in maintaining contact for more than a year or two. . . . In general, long-lasting friendships are comparatively rare" (65). Unlike marriage where, until recently at least (and still in the great majority of cases), one partner moved with the other, in friendship, no one would expect a friend to move with him. Not least among the complex effects of this migratory fact of life is an increased desire to certify a relationship's genuineness quickly, and this may well have something to do with the impatient attempt to circumvent forms and the related earnestness about establishing authenticity.

I think Aristotle is being quite literal when he refers to "living in each other's company," but I would argue that it is possible to do so even when one lives in a different town. For there is physical distance and there is psychic or spiritual distance, and today, in a society in which a fifth of the people move out of town every five years (to say nothing of social and economic moves), it is scarcely possible to maintain most friendships unless one becomes adept at long distance calls. Not long ago, separated friends kept in touch through letters; in fact, there is now a whole genre of collections of letters that record friendships. The primary medium today, however, is the telephone.

This fact has not been lost on Ma Bell, with her shrewd appeal for us to "reach out and touch someone." These ads used to show children calling parents or grandparents, or lovers calling lovers, but lately one sees middle-aged men calling old buddies and reminiscing about childhood, women in their late twenties calling old roommates, or older women talking to long-standing friends.

Nor is it easy to keep friendships alive over the long distance lines. In some relationships one can simply not find a way of talking intimately at all, whereas in others, one cannot find a way of chatting congenially, which is just as important in these situations as direct intimate exchange. Negotiating that balance is difficult, for the scales can be excruciatingly sensitive to nuance and rhythm. I had one friendship that foundered mainly because we never found the means to reestablish our mutual regard and affection on the long distance telephone. Our silences were awkward but no more so than our clumsy attempts to speak intimately, to ask and tell each other how we were *"really* doing." These ended up like botched raids on foreign territory, and they did so because of what I regard as a creative lapse: we were unable to generate those formal means, those extraordinarily complicated games that friends must both invent and successfully play if they are to keep their friendships alive.

After roughly a decade in the academic world my other friend—my childhood friend—and I were still wondering how seriously to take ourselves. We were adults now, even parents, and we used to play a game with his first child in which we would ask, "How big is Jen?" She would raise her two-year-old arms to show us how big and we would move in for the tickle. As we began to publish articles and then books, we continued our comic routine about being "big," so that one night when I answered my phone I heard a faint voice asking, "You big?"

"Sure I'm big. You?" (I hadn't hesitated a split second and my pitch was perfect.)

"Yeah, I'm big."

"How big?" I asked, voice rising.

"Big!" he bellowed.

"I mean, your book's been well reviewed but are you a guy who wrote a good book or are you *big?"*

We went on like this for a while, never breaking from our assumed roles, never missing a line, and delivering our speeches with the skill of experienced actors. For a quarter of an hour we performed this formal dance, weaving in and out of our own brand of irony and solemnity, silliness and seriousness. There is no reason to provide further details because in one sense, as with certain comic situations, you had to be there. But what followed in that conversation was one of the most important talks I have ever had. It was truly a conversation in which both of us were exploring, hypothesizing, testing, and validating our experiences, our values, our aspirations, and our sense of ourselves.

Both of us had been privately assessing ourselves and the direction of our lives and ambitions, and both of us had realized that we were no longer strangers in that world that, not so long ago, had seemed so alien. But could it be that we were not only at home in that world now but actually among its proprietors or shapers? We talked about the most intimate matters of our careers, our families, our dreams and our fears, but we rarely talked about them directly. Our conversation was as distinct from the stereotypical intimate conversation between friends as anything I can imagine, but it was profoundly intimate nonetheless. We joked, we cajoled, we teased, we playacted, we confessed, we defended, and we queried. We were able to discern the shape, the status, perhaps even something of the fate of our hopes and our emerging sense of ourselves by interpreting a thousand intonations and pauses, for we had developed a language of extraordinary complexity and richness, and not least among the charged semantic units of that language was the word *big*. Like Jennifer, we too were growing up, or continuing to grow up, and in the playground of our friendship we were performing the kind of rehearsal that characterizes so much of play, for adults as well as children. One could risk exposing one's new sense of oneself in front of a friend, particularly when one of the unspoken rules of the "big" game was that we both did and did not take ambition seriously. We honored worldly success and we encouraged each other to pursue it, but we also felt it was transient and insignificant compared with the permanent and ultimately meaningful bond of our friendship. The friend is the one with whom we can play out that simultaneous perception of the value and triviality of the public. He is also the one who will somehow let us know if the new self we present is consistent with the former repertoire he knows so well. He will be able to identify and accept change but he will measure it against some sense of identity over time, and he will thus, as Robert Louis Stevenson puts it, "keep us worthy of ourselves" (187).

To put the matter in this way is to suggest both a metaphysical and an ethical dimension of friendship, for the friend not only validates and concretizes one's sense of identity and reality; he also in one way or another evaluates it. A similar teleological conception of friendship can be seen in the Old Testament proverb, "Iron sharpeneth iron; / So a man sharpeneth the countenance of his friend."[8] The process by which we help our friends become what they are can be best understood as a process of play, in the sense that James Hans uses that word in *The Play of the World*. "The role of play is not to work comfortably within its own structures," says Hans, "but rather constantly to develop its structures through play" (5)—which is what my friend and I did with the "big" game. As with the hermeneutic circle, according to Hans, "play begins with the putting-in-question, and proceeds, ideally, until some further understanding of that which has been put into question has been achieved" (8). This describes perfectly what happened on that long distance call, as does Hans's claim that "man may have a purpose in his play, but this purpose is always no more than an orientation if his play really is to be play" (32). Had my friend called me *in order* to have a serious conversation about the matters we ended up discussing, we would have had a much tougher go of it. The importance of that talk had much to do with the fact that we were playing hard at the game of friendship rather than trying to break through the forms to an imagined and chimerical aformal direct intimacy. We had invented a game of great subtlety; had learned, without ever speaking, its rules; and had adapted it to our most urgent, if not wholly conscious, purposes.

"At one level," says Hans, "novelty and repetition—and the play between them—determine the context of play, for play clearly needs them both. . . . All play shares one thing with games: a familiar structure that allows one to play with the unfamiliar. . . . Nor is this familiar structure always the same. Indeed, it changes every time it is played with" (28). This all seems to me very much to the point—not only for the phone call I have described in detail but more generally for friendship itself. It may seem odd to use the words *game* and *play* here because to many ears they have the ring of whatever is *opposed* to the serious, and clearly I mean these words to describe the most serious of experiences and categories. "It is one of the difficult and delightful subtleties of life," says C. S. Lewis in *The Four Loves,* "that we must deeply acknowledge certain things to be serious and yet retain the power and will to treat them often as lightly as a game" (105). "Man only plays," says Friedrich Schiller, "when he is in the fullest sense of the word a human being, and he is only fully a human being when he plays" (107).

Play and games have recently been the subject of considerable philosophical discussion, but for our purposes the central point is play's similarity to art and ritual. Like them, play has rules, which are sometimes followed, sometimes violated, and sometimes rewritten. Like them, it employs the symbolic, even in the children's game in which "this chair's the castle and you're the bad guy." But play is not related to art and ritual only in its formal and symbolic structure; it also, like them, operates with a delicate dialectic between illusion and reality and between creation and criticism. Like them, it constructs realities, interprets them, and evaluates them in one continuous process. In the example of my long distance phone conversation, the game that my friend and I developed and successfully played can be seen as analogous to a work of art in the sense that both handle an extraordinary complex of experience in such a way as to realign its component parts, at least, and reshape it altogether, at best. In these terms, friendship might be understood as a relationship in which two people want to play together and do in fact play well together and enjoy their play.

The last element, enjoyment, is as crucial and undervalued in friendship as it is (to continue the analogy) in art. Cicero, more than anyone else, seems to have understood just how important congeniality is, and he seems to have Aristotle's perhaps excessively sober concern with virtue in mind when he offers a corrective. "People speak of rectitude," says Cicero, "and of an all-pervading seriousness; the latter, to be sure, does impart solidity, but friendship must be more relaxed and less constricting and more pleasurable, and more inclined to affability and congeniality in all aspects" (75). There is an interesting paradox here, for although it is true that one feels most relaxed with a friend, one also feels most excited. That paradoxical combination of relaxation and excitement is not unlike the one we find in the finest moments of experiences as diverse as sports and sex.

Wordsworth tells us in *The Prelude* that "Genius [is] born to thrive by interchange / Of peace and excitation" (13.5–6). Friendship, I would suggest, also thrives by that interchange, or perhaps, more accurately, that merging. "The feeling of friendship," says James Boswell, "is like that of being comfortably filled with roast beef" as opposed to that of love, which is "like being enlivened with champagne" (624).[9] There is indeed something easy and comfortable about friendship, and yet, though Boswell surely has a point about being comfortably filled, he might with equal aptness have used a good salad to distinguish it from love's champagne. We do not feel drunk or giddy in friendship but neither do we feel merely well fed and content, like sleepy uncles after a holiday meal. Dr. Johnson seems to have had precisely this distinction in mind in his response to Boswell's observation. "No, Sir," says Johnson; "love [is] like being intoxicated with champagne; . . . friendship like being enlivened" (624). Our comfort, that is to say, is combined with a buoyant sense of energy and vitality. Our friends do not keep us on edge but they do keep our edge on us.

The comfortable quality of friendship provides a kind of tranquillity and it consoles us at difficult times, but the intensity is what magnifies our joys and makes everything somehow finer and more delightful when we are in a friend's company.[10] Bacon suggests that even our thinking is better when we are with a friend. A friend's "wits and understanding," he says, "do clarify and break up in the communicating and discoursing with [his friend]; he tosseth his thoughts more easily; he marshalleth them more orderly; he seeth how they look when they are turned into words; finally, he waxeth wiser than himself; and that more by an hour's discourse than by a day's meditation" (79). But what is it that makes possible this facility for bringing our own thoughts to light when we are talking with a friend? Not the least of friendship's paradoxes is that it allows us to be simultaneously relaxed and excited.

That conjunction of emotions is certainly one reason why friendship—or any play—is enjoyable. Another crucial reason is to be found in friendship's relation to the comic. Evelyn Waugh may distort the matter when he says "we cherish our friends not for their ability to amuse us, but for ours to amuse them" (qtd. in Peter 214). But he is right to emphasize the importance of amusement in friendship. One thinks immediately of Shakespeare's Prince Hal, whose disarming élan is distinguished from Hotspur's mainly by virtue of his love of laughter. Hotspur, for all his highblown notions of honor and chivalry, is unqualified for friendship—and indeed, Shakespeare suggests, for statesmanship—partly because he is so humorless. Hal, on the other hand, has an exquisite sense of both the advantages and limitations of role-playing, so that it would be equally inaccurate to say that he is friends with Falstaff despite Falstaff's limitations (Hal does, after all, betray him), or that he befriends him because of them. Like the friends I described earlier, Hal can sustain a dual perception of the claims of the public and the private; he knows that at some level Falstaff is as worthy as Hotspur.

To put the matter in this way is to suggest that friendship often carries with it an implicit critique of society. That, in fact, is one of friendship's central comic features. For comedy always poses an alternative world, whether it is one of Shakespeare's fairylands or forests, or the vision of another configuration of reality off which a simple joke plays. Henri Bergson claims that the "natural environment" of laughter is society, and that "our laughter is always the laughter of a group. . . . However spontaneous it seems, laughter always implies a kind of secret freemasonry, or even complicity with other laughters, real or imaginary. . . . Many comic effects are incapable of translation from one language to another, because they refer to the customs and ideas of a particular social group!" (64–65).

One kind of social group—the smallest kind—is a friendship, which surely has its own customs and ideas as well as its own language. Indeed, one of our most common ways of describing a successful friendship is to say that we "speak the same language," and by that we refer to a vast array of languages, from hand gesture to intonation, from allusion to rhythm, and far beyond into the awesome density of coding that we call body language. Friends can decipher these endlessly complex codes in a split second because they have mastered the rules of their friendship's language; they have become experts at playing a complicated and serious game. " 'Twixt such friends as we / Few words suffice," says Petruchio to Hortensio in *The Taming of the Shrew* (1.2.64–65). With close friends, a single word, a gesture, a tone of voice, even a silence can speak volumes. A friendship has its own history, its own founding, its own civil and foreign wars, its own mythic events, its own status quo, its own vision of the future, its own ethos, ideals, and legal system. It has, that is to say, not only a language but a culture in the sense that Trilling uses that term to describe "a unitary complex of interacting assumptions, modes of thought, habits, and styles, which are connected in secret as well as overt ways with the practical arrangements of a society" (125). We might as accurately say that a friendship is both a language and a culture, and that to be able to speak and understand its language, its citizens must have learned what it is like to live in that miniature culture.

Clearly there is no clean line that marks off the culture of a particular friendship from that of another, or from the larger society in which they exist. In fact, a good deal of the culture of a friendship in these terms will be determined by that larger culture. But it is the point of differentiation rather than similarity that concerns us here, for in one sense a friendship is a kind of private shelter from the demands of the public. It somehow concretizes the world and gives a solid, palpable feel to reality, as Emily Dickinson suggests in one of her poems:

> The Day she goes
> Or Day she stays
> Are equally supreme—
> Existence has a stated width
> Departed, or at Home—
> (Number 1308, 3:908)

Friendship is also a more comfortable home, in the sense that we feel more fully "housed" in the society of our friendship than we do in the larger culture. As Dickinson says of her friend:

> Her heart is fit for *home*—
> I—a sparrow—build there
> Sweet of twigs and twine
> My perennial nest.
> (Number 84, 1:69)

This is partly a question of scope and scale, but the key point is that one feels more familiar, more comfortable (in Boswell's sense of being filled with hearty beef) precisely because one is more fluent in this language than in the other, because one plays so much better here than there. This culture, after all, was the friends' own creation. "The bird a nest," says Blake in *The Marriage of Heaven and Hell,* "the spider a web, man friendship" (8.31). That network of connecting threads is both our creation and our home.

There are times, of course, when the two cultures come into conflict. "If I had to choose between betraying my country and betraying my friend," says E. M. Forster, "I hope I should have the guts to betray my country" (66). Such a choice might at first seem shocking, but it would not, says Forster, have repelled Dante, who, he reminds us, "places Brutus and Cassius in the lowest circle of Hell because they had chosen to betray their friend Julius Caesar rather than their country Rome" (66).[11] Without examining the complex moral issues here, we can at least remark the power of the claims made by the culture of friendship.

That power makes itself felt in less dramatic contexts as well. For example, to the extent that one does feel more at home in the alternative society of friendship, one may become increasingly aware of the limitations of the larger culture, and one's shared perspective on it may become the stuff of comedy.[12] The critique needn't be fierce—often it is gentle and usually it is tacit—but it always plays off its differentiation of itself and its values from those of the larger society. We can even see this principle operating at the level of the joke, whose "excitement," says Brain, "lies in the suggestion that any particular ordering of experience or society may be arbitrary. It provides an opportunity for a sudden intuitive realization that an accepted pattern is not necessary. . . . The joke . . . says something of value about individuals as against the value of social relations and community" (181). The joke, I would add, also says something of value about the shared understanding of the friends as against that of the social system.

This is one reason jokes are often so important in a friendship: they affirm the legitimacy of the private league that the friendship constitutes. They sanction both our need to play in a smaller game and our sense that that game may be the most important one. But as Brain points out, joking relationships are also "ambivalent, since a taboo on being offended by the coarsest of insults makes it obviously impossible for conflict to arise while at the same time joking stresses the intimacy between partners" (186). Brain suggests that "a rowdy display of horseplay" between friends operates in a similar fashion, expressing "the element of strain and fragility in all friendships" (11). Both "allow love to persist without shame and may also betray a latent sentiment of aggression which is not always absent from loving relationships" (11).

I have occasionally found myself in the situation of teasing a close friend unmercifully in the company of another person who does not know us—or our friendship—very well. The other person becomes more and more embarrassed as I heap on the insults, and he thinks we are having a fight when my friend begins to reciprocate. What the outsider does not know, of course, is that my friend and I are playing an old game whose primary rule is precisely the one Brain has in mind when he refers to "a taboo on being offended by the coarsest of insults." What is most fascinating about this game—and what most mystifies the poor souls who have never played it— is that it is the friends' intimacy and trust, not conflict and distance, that are being affirmed. The game is scarcely sentimental, for like most teasing it is based on the assumption that, as Brain says, there is an "element of strain and fragility in all friendships." This game recognizes that fact not by repressing it, but by engaging it in meaningful play and thereby domesticating it. The taboo against being offended is a way of saying that the friendship can survive its inevitable strain; the insulting game is a formal strategy that the friends employ (though not consciously) as a way of showing themselves that their friendship is stronger than their own worst impulses; it is a drama they stage for their own benefit.[13]

When Brain claims that there is an "element of strain and fragility in *all* friendships" (emphasis mine), he carefully qualifies his claim about the "latent sentiment of aggression." That, he says "is *not always absent* from loving relationships" (emphasis mine). I suppose Freud and Konrad Lorenz would disapprove of Brain's qualifications, but we needn't involve ourselves in the elaborate debate about aggression and love to observe that whether or not Brain has unnecessarily qualified his assertion, it is true. Few would dispute the claim that "a latent sentiment of aggression . . . is not always absent from loving relationships." The crucial issue for friendship is not whether we are fundamentally aggressive creatures but rather how we handle what aggression we have.

In the example of the insulting game that I described earlier, whatever aggression was present was not only controlled; it was actually put to the service of the bond of intimacy. We see the constructive channeling of aggression at work in a more blatant way in the teasing, the tender insults, and mock anger that occasionally provide the unusual means for friends to make up after a quarrel. The conjunction of aggression and games follows an interesting pattern in the history of friendship. Brain does not observe this conjunction or the historical pattern, but he does refer to an institution that for our purposes provides a perfect illustration. In the feudal period, Brain points out, one sent a boy "to be 'fostered' in the household of one's overlord, where he learnt manners and was trained in arms, horsemanship, and sports. Two young men thus growing up side by side . . . and competing together in games would become special friends . . . and this intimacy and rivalry continued throughout their lives as warriors" (30). In this instance the rivalry is built into the relationship from the outset, as though to prepare one for what in one form or another is inevitable anyhow. The institutionalization of the rivalry in games is a more straightforward way of providing what we saw in the joking relationship and the insult game. Brain tells us that among "the most striking aspects of these warriors was their formal courtesy: in grief or in fondness, in fighting and in dying, the mode of address is always 'fair sir, companion . . .'" (30). The movement from formal courtesy in the medieval period to informal familiarity in our own is clear enough, but the more important point is that, as in most other matters of friendship, the movement is accompanied by a shift from social institutions to private ones, from public games to private ones.

We can observe a similar pattern if we compare another medieval practice to a modern one. Malory describes knights choosing friends by finding worthy foes on the battlefield. Today we retain an uninstitutionalized version of this practice in our conception of "healthy competition," a principle we can see more literally in the common practice of friends competing against each other in sports, and more indirectly in, say, the battles of wit that often go on between friends. In these instances one's friend keeps one on one's toes, keeps one fit, as it were, for his company.

"In the adversity of our best friends," says La Rochefoucauld, "we always find something which does not displease us" (qtd. in B. Stevenson 736). La Rochefoucauld was not always as cynical about friendship as he was in this most famous of his maxims on the subject, and indeed, he is less cynical than Henry Adams, who coyly suggests that "friendship needs a certain parallelism of life, a community of thought, a rivalry of aim" (312). At least La Rochefoucauld does not preclude the possibility that a friendship might survive—even flourish— despite whatever competition might arise as a result of having an equality, not a rivalry, of aim. Still, the idea of healthy competition remains an ideal that is not always easy to live up to, and competition more often than not proves to be an insoluble problem, rather than a component, of friendship. We certainly do see it when we confront our friend's bad fortune but it seems to me that we see it more frequently—and insidiously—when we confront his good fortune. No proverb about friendship in the Anglo-American tradition is more common than the various versions of "a friend in need is a friend indeed." Clearly, the weight of this proverbial wisdom reflects a clear sense in our culture that the most important defining feature of a friend is that he is someone to whom we can turn in difficult times. All of the great essays on friendship take up this theme, but most of them also emphasize that a friend is someone with whom we can share our joys. Dr. Johnson tells us a friend must "not only be firm in the day of distress, but gay in the hour of jollity," for it is "necessary that friends partake each others pleasures as well as cares" (342–43). Cicero knows that friends help us bear misfortune but he also asks, "How could you derive true joy from good fortune, if you did not have someone who would rejoice in your happiness as much as you yourself?" (55). Aristotle lays his emphasis squarely on sharing our joys. "Is the need of friends greater in good fortune or in bad?" he asks, and he concludes that "friends are more indispensable in bad fortune. . . . But it is nobler to have friends in good fortune." While "it is perhaps fitting for a man to go unasked and eagerly to a friend in misfortune," we should "be reluctant to ask our friend to share our misfortunes." In the opposite case, however, "it is . . . fitting to join eagerly in the activities of a friend who is enjoying good fortune" and "we ought to be eager to invite our friends to share our good fortunes" (269–71). Nietzsche goes furthest: "Fellowship in joy, and not sympathy in sorrow, makes people friends" (*Human* 358).

I quote these passages because they remind us that we diminish friendship if we think of it mostly as a kind of crisis insurance. I think that has been the recent tendency in our culture, most obviously, perhaps, in the development of encounter groups but also in our general concept of friendship. The ability genuinely to share the joys of another is rare; envy is a familiar emotion, even with friends. All of us have had the experience of telling a friend some good news—a new love, a new job, a promotion, a child's success—only to hear a slight pause or see a sudden wince that speaks volumes before the friend replies, in a sinking voice, "Wonderful, wonderful." Conversely, we might overhear in our own voice, as we share our good news, a certain gloating that is quite different from the sound of genuine excitement, as though our real satisfaction were not in the good fortune itself but in the fact that it happened to us and not our friend.

This is the raw material of maxims; one can imagine a dozen fine ones in the manner of La Rochefoucauld. But the mere presence of competition or bad feeling in friendship does not mean that the friendship is inauthentic or doomed. No doubt there have been friendships in which no aggression or competition was present, but in most friendships—and I include in this category most noble friendships—aggression and competition are not absent but tamed. Recall, for a moment, that long distance call I described. The "big" game not only focused a mutual concern about ambition; it also gave play to our spirit of competition, for in addition to measuring ourselves against others, we were taking the measure of one another. Nor was this to ill effect; on the contrary, it strengthened our friendship because, like the joking game that gives vent to conflict or the insult game that gives vent to aggression, this game gave vent to our sense of competition. To the extent that we played the game successfully, we preserved the salutary side of our competition (the sense in which it kept us alert and eager to be and do the best of which we were capable) and we purged the crude and more self-interested side.

Of course friends are not always so lucky. In many cases the competition proves too much and it overwhelms and destroys whatever good feelings remain. In one sense, I think, Nietzsche is right: the best way to find out who your true friends are is not to see who consoles you in your sorrow but to see who really is able to share your joy. Some people simply cannot deal with the successes of their friends. When confronted with such a situation, one may keep one's successes to oneself, report them in an anxious tone that the friend mistakes for gloating, or relate them with an innocent enthusiasm that is also mistaken for gloating. One is made to feel that one's true joy is not so much in getting promoted as in showing up one's friend. No friendship can survive the kind of mutual resentment that grows here.

To regard friendship mainly—or only—as crisis insurance is somehow to relegate it to the position it holds in the old English proverb, "A true friend shall be like a privy, open in necessity" (qtd. in Tilley 245). But it is also true that crisis insurance is one of its important functions. One turns to a friend when there is death, illness, divorce, financial hardship, or emotional upheaval. In this connection we now hear a good deal about "support systems" and "networks," particularly for women. But in the mid–nineteenth century Elizabeth Gaskell was already documenting with remarkable sensitivity precisely such systems. *Cranford,* her immensely popular novel originally serialized in Dickens's journal *Household Words* and published in 1853, is set in a village of that name in England. Though Cranford is home to some married people, a few widows, and even fewer men, most of its inhabitants are spinsters. Gaskell explores the lives of these women by taking them through a series of adventures and by observing how they respond to major and minor calamities.

The social life of Cranford is regulated by explicit rules:

> Then there were rules and regulations for visiting and calls; and they were announced to any young people, who might be staying in the town, with all the solemnity with which the old Manx laws were read once a year on the Tinwald Mount. . . .
>
> "I dare say your mamma has told you, my dear, never to let more than three days elapse between receiving a call and returning it; and also, that you are never to stay longer than a quarter of an hour."
>
> "But am I to look at my watch? How am I to find out when a quarter of an hour has passed?"
>
> "You must keep thinking about the time, my dear, and not allow yourself to forget it in conversation."
>
> As everybody had this rule in their minds, whether they received or paid a call, of course no absorbing subject was ever spoken about. We kept ourselves to short sentences of small talk, and were punctual to our time. (40–41)

The atmosphere sounds not only claustrophobic but positively stifling.

"None of us spoke of money," the narrator tell us, "because that subject savoured of commerce and trade, and though some might be poor, we were all aristocratic" (41). This pretense, actually based on the fact that money was scarce, takes a number of forms. Mary and Miss Matty can afford to burn only one candle at night, but "as we lived in constant preparation for a friend who might come in any evening (but who never did), it required some contrivance to keep our two candles of the same length, ready to be lighted, and to look as if we burnt two always" (84). Rules for visiting friends are bad enough; they seem to us the very antithesis of the kind of spontaneity that ought to govern friendships. But this pretense seems even worse for it appears to reveal the friendships as inauthentic at the core. What emerges is a picture of friendships so regulated by protocol that they lose their spontaneous engine and putter along in the dust of hypocrisy and obligation. That picture seems part of a larger, more stereotypical Victorian picture: " 'It is very pleasant dining with a bachelor,' said Miss Matty, softly. . . . 'I only hope it is not improper; so many pleasant things are!' " (75).

Gaskell does a magnificent job stacking the deck in this way during the early part of the novel, and in the process she prepares us to look with scorn—or, more accurately, condescending humor—on the friendships that unfold. But the remainder of the novel reverses our expectations brilliantly, and in so doing it forces us to reconsider our facile understanding of the relationship between form and friendship. The pivotal event occurs when the old woman, Matty, loses all her money, and the other women, themselves in a pinch, find a way to help her. The chapter, appropriately, is called "Friends in Need." Miss Poole addresses the group:

> "We, the ladies of Cranford, in my drawing room assembled, can resolve upon something. . . . and one and all of us have agreed that, while we have a superfluity, it is not only a duty but a pleasure,—a true pleasure, Mary!"—her voice was rather choked just here, and she had to wipe her spectacles before she could go on—"to give what we can to assist her—Miss Matilda Jenkyns. Only, in consideration of the feelings of delicate independence existing in the mind of every refined female. . . . —we wish to contribute our mites in a secret and concealed manner, so as not to hurt the feelings I have referred to. And our object in requesting you to meet us this morning, is, that believing . . . that your father is, in fact, her confidential adviser in all pecuniary matters, we imagined that, by consulting with him, you might devise some mode in which our contribution could be made to appear the legal due which Miss Matilda Jenkyns ought to receive from ———. Probably, your father, knowing her investments, can fill up the blank." (191–92)

The narrator goes on:

> The worst was, all the ladies cried in concert. Even Miss Poole cried, who had said a hundred times that to betray emotion before any one was a sign of weakness and want of self-control. She recovered herself into a slight degree of impatient anger, directed against me, as having set them all off. (192)

The circumstances of their lives require considerable emotional self-control. This scene is poignant precisely because that control has been in force: its violation now suggests both the intensity and the authenticity of the compassion. With any form, interruption of a regular pattern carries more significance than random positioning. When an accomplished poet deviates from the metrical pattern he has established, he does so for a reason, and the deviation is immediately thrown into relief by the regularity of the form. When Miss Poole betrays emotion, we know it is real. Form in this instance serves rather than obstructs sincerity.

No one knew this better or put it to more elaborate literary use than Jane Austen. Even in her earliest work, *Love and Friendship,* she satirizes the sentimental view that love and friendship exist outside of formal structures and thrive only on spontaneity, "Delicate feeling, tender Sentiments, and refined Sensibility" (17). Edward and Augustus, Sophia and Laura fall in love and form friendships as quickly as you or I might settle on a particular loaf of bread at the bakery. "After having been deprived during the course of 3 weeks of a real friend," says Laura in reference to her first meeting with Sophia, "imagine my transports at beholding one, most truly worthy of the Name. . . . She was all Sensibility and Feeling. We flew into each others arms and after having exchanged vows of mutual Friendship for the rest of our Lives, instantly unfolded to each other the most inward Secrets of our Hearts—" (19–20).

Except for the part about "the rest of our Lives," this scene—especially the attempt at instant intimacy and confession—might well have taken place at any of a thousand American singles bars. Unlike lovers, who conventionally de-clare their love, friends in our culture rarely tell each other of their friendly feelings, either to establish the friendship or to reassure each other. The risk of sentimentality is so much greater with friendship. Lovers somehow have more license for sentimentality; friends more readily sound like Sydney Smith: "Madam, I have been looking for a person who disliked gravy all my life; let us swear eternal friendship" (Holland 307). The pretentious formality here is bad enough, to say nothing of the triviality of the object. But is there much difference, finally, between this avowal and that proposed by Adelaide Bry in her recent self-help book on friendship? Bry recommends that when you meet someone you like, you should "look your Potential Friend straight in the eye and . . . say simply, 'Hey, you and I have a lot in common. I like you. I'd like to be friends'" (39).

Austen exposes precisely this kind of naïveté in the rest of Laura's speech. "In the Society of my Edward & this Amiable Pair," she says, "I passed the happiest moments of my Life: Our time was most delightfully spent, in mutual Protestations of Freindship [sic] and in vows of unalterable Love, in which we were secure from being interrupted, by intruding & disagreeable Visitors, as Augustus & Sophia had on their first Entrance in the Neighborhood, taken due care to inform the surrounding Families, that as their Happiness centered wholly in themselves, they wished for no other society" (22–23).

The humor here, as so often in satire, results from the gap between appearance and reality: friendship, sincerity, and intimacy cannot, we know, be magically summoned into being by histrionic gestures. But the view that is being satirized is one whose whole *raison d'être* is to overcome the gap between appearance and reality. These characters see themselves as having escaped rigid social conventions. They especially relish attacks on parental authority, but they delight in even the most trivial affront to polite behavior. The deepest comedy here issues from Austen's insight that they have merely replaced one set of conventions with another. Their ignorance of this fact leads to a particularly absurd self-righteousness, as when they meet Graham: "They said he was Sensible, well-informed, and Agreeable; we did not pretend to Judge of such trifles, but as we were convinced he had no soul, that he had never read the Sorrows of Werter, & that his Hair bore not the slightest resemblance to Auburn, we were certain Janetta could feel no affection for him, or at least that she ought to feel none" (34–35).

The reference to Goethe's *The Sorrows of Young Werther* recalls a whole literary tradition of sentimentality which can now be seen as a highly wrought system of conventions. Sincerity, freedom from form, open avowal and great intensity of feeling—these are its hallmarks, and Austen satirizes them all brilliantly, showing them to be just as subject to form and convention as the most rigid set of social regulations. Forms are not themselves confining and deadening, Austen suggests. They do not inevitably lead to obligation, pretense, and hypocrisy, and we must not, therefore, assume that spontaneity, freedom, openness, and sincerity are to be found *outside* of forms. All of Austen's work suggests that the issue is not how to circumvent forms but how to use them creatively.[14]

If we return to *Cranford,* we can begin to see this principle operating in interesting ways. After the ladies had cried,

> paper, pens, and ink were provided. Every lady wrote down the sum she could give annually, signed the paper, and sealed it mysteriously. . . .
>
> On coming downstairs I found Mrs. Forrester waiting for me . . . the poor old lady trembling all the time as if it were a great crime which she was exposing to daylight, in telling me how very, very little she had to live upon; a confession which she was brought to make from a dread lest we should think that the small contribution named in her paper bore any proportion to her love and regard for Miss Matty. And yet that sum which she so eagerly relinquished was, in truth, more than a twentieth part of what she had to live upon, and keep house, and a little serving-maid, all as became one born a Tyrrell. And when the whole income does not nearly amount to a hundred pounds, to give up a twentieth of it will necessitate many careful economies, and many pieces of self-denial—small and insignificant in the world's ac-

count, but bearing a different value in another account-book that I have heard of. She did so wish she was rich, she said; and this wish she kept repeating, with no thought of herself in it, only with a longing, yearning desire to be able to heap up Miss Matty's measure of comforts.

It was some time before I could console her enough to leave (192–93)

It is true that Mrs. Forrester is worried that the other women will misinterpret her small donation as stinginess, but it is equally true that her generosity is genuine. Her social concern does not preclude her generosity; if anything, it intensifies it. The women improvised this form to preserve Matty's dignity and livelihood, but it also provided a vehicle for the community to express its solidarity. Who can say whether the deepest motive for the compassion and self-sacrifice was altruistic or self-interested? At some level, certainly, it must have been reassuring for these vulnerable women to see each other rallying to the defense of one of their number, for one might soon find oneself in a similar situation of need. Not even the most altruistic point of view would deny that one important function of society—even a society of two—is mutual protection, or, as we said earlier, crisis insurance. The point of all the talk we hear today about support systems is that friendship is something we can fall back on in a pinch. But the question still remains whether one undertakes acts of friendship out of a genuine concern for one's friend or out of a concealed self-regard. Do the women of Cranford come to Matty's aid because they truly feel compassion for her or because at some primordial level of social consciousness they know that doing so will guarantee their own safety and security?

Here we confront the whole vexed question of altruism, which has been complicated even further by recent controversies over sociobiology. Though we can hardly provide a definitive answer to this quetsion, we can say that Gaskell seems to incline to the view that altruistic feelings do indeed exist. Mrs. Poole, we remember, repeated her wish to be rich "with no thought of herself in it, only with a longing, yearning desire to be able to heap up Miss Matty's measure of comforts." The excessive repetition might betray self-concern, but even if altruistic feelings coexist with more self-interested motives, they are central, for Gaskell, to her characters' actions. It is possible, that is to say, for the women to be both altruistic and self-interested. "To say that an act is altruistic," says Lawrence A. Blum in *Friendship, Altruism and Morality*, "is only to say that it involves and is motivated by a genuine regard for another's welfare; it is not to say that in performing it the agent neglects his own interests and desires" (10). As with aggression and competition, we needn't deny the existence of all self-interest here to affirm the presence of genuine friendship.

The point applies not only to the motives for undertaking a particular act of friendship but also to the motives for entering a friendship in the first place. According to Cicero, the origin of friendship is not human weakness but strength; one does not undertake a true friendship out of a desire for help or dependence but out of "love (*amor*), the thing that gives us our word for friendship (*amicitia*), that provides the first impulse toward mutual regard . . . an inclination of the heart together with a feeling of affection rather than . . . a consideration of the advantages which we might derive" (58). For Cicero, one does not enter a friendship in order to "fulfill needs" or seek advantages. One's needs are in fact fulfilled in a friendship and one does in fact derive benefits from a friendship, but that is not why one undertakes it.

The point is worth laboring, for the distinction is crucial. The major interpretive forms of our century have explained human phenomena by analyzing their origins, by locating their roots in the genes, the unconscious, the economy, the environment, or in mere self-interest. This is one among many reasons why friendship has been so widely ignored in our recent literature, for this kind of reductive analysis can scarcely provide an adequate account of the ways in which we create ourselves and each other in friendships. Is there competition in the friendship? Aha—impure at the root. Aggression?

Fundamental hostility masquerading as affability. And is it not in Miss Poole's own interest to come to the aid of Miss Matty? So much for benevolence.

Friendship has had a hard go of it, for it has been distorted by both ends of a conceptual spectrum ranging from saccharine sentimentality to reductive cynicism. The sentimental view, which Austen satirizes so brilliantly, is based on the assumption that friendship moves and breathes in a realm of pure ether, utterly free from the sublunar corruptions of competition, aggression, and self-interest. The cynical view operates on the equally erroneous assumption that having identified the presence of these pollutants, we have both provided a sufficient explanation of friendship and discredited its pretensions. But those tired old formulas that discover base motives beneath exalted feelings and ideals are by now the stock and trade of any sophomore. No one would dispute the claim that the rose is rooted in dung, but neither would one accept that observation as an exhaustive explanation of the rose. To claim that friendship often involves competition, aggression, and self-interest does not discredit friendship; it merely states the obvious. The important questions are how friends find ways of protecting themselves against these liabilities and how, in some cases, they transform them into assets.

To our list of aggression, competition, and self-interest we might add secrecy or lack of openness as another quality that seems to—but may not in fact—be inimical to friendship. In *Cranford,* when Mary hears that Thomas Hollbrook, Matty's fiancé, does not have long to live, she asks Miss Poole:

> "Does Miss Matilda know of his illness?" . . . —a new light as to the cause of her indisposition dawning on me.
>
> "Dear! to be sure, yes! Has not she told you? I let her know a fortnight ago, or more, when I first heard of it. How odd she shouldn't have told you!"
>
> Not at all, I thought; but I did not say anything. I felt almost guilty of having spied too curiously into that

tender heart, and I was not going to speak of its secrets, —hidden, Miss Matty believed, from all the world (80).

When Hollbrook died, "Miss Matty made a strong effort to conceal her feelings—a concealment she practised even with me . . ." (81). Clearly Matty's secrecy has something to do with the painfulness of even raising the subject. But isn't this precisely the kind of situation in which one can—and should—talk to a friend? Cicero, we recall, says that "in friendship there can be no element of show or pretense; everything in it is honest and spontaneous" (58). Bacon goes even further: "Certainly if a man would give it a hard phrase, those that want [i.e., lack] friends to open themselves unto are cannibals of their own hearts" (78). Miss Matty is scarcely an emotional cannibal, particularly of her own heart, which Mary describes as "tender." Nor is Mary surprised that Matty has concealed her grief. This seems to be a characteristic act on Matty's part and it reveals a sense of privacy that may now seem alien to us but to Mary seemed worthy of respect.

We draw a fine line between our condemnation of privacy and our admiration of it, particularly in circumstances of misfortune. The one we call foolish or stubborn; the other, dignified or brave. Rose Kennedy, I suppose, remains our model of the latter. She did not publicly indulge her grief over her fallen sons; we sensed she felt it intensely but she fulfilled her public obligations all the same, and with a dignity of bearing that most Americans seemed to admire. On a drastically smaller scale and assuming the analogy of culture and friendship that I outlined earlier, Miss Matty's refusal to share her grief with her friend dramatizes the same complex of issues. How far should one inflict one's pain on one's friends? At what point, or in what situations, do attempts to get closer to a friend actually violate his privacy? Is there an inherent tension between intimacy and privacy?

In the case of Mary and Matty, a number of points are clear. In the first place, Matty obeys Aristotle's injunction that true friends should "take scrupulous care not to let their friends share their pain" for we should "avoid being the cause of a friend's pain" (270). Second, there can be no question of the authenticity of Matty's feelings or the nature of her motives. Her concealment, far from suggesting any deception or hypocrisy, stems from genuine concern for Mary and their relationship. Mary realizes this and is moved by it. Matty's concealment, it turns out, is the very agent of intimacy, not its opponent.

If concealment can be the agent of intimacy, so, paradoxically, can distance create closeness. I had a letter recently from a prominent anthropologist who was describing her oldest and closest friendship. A few years ago, she said, her friend went to England for the summer and she wrote her a letter there. The friend wrote back and gradually they discovered a new dimension of communication in their relationship. When the friend returned, they continued the correspondence for another two years even though they now lived only a mile apart, and saw each other almost every day. Occasionally they actually wrote to each other even while they were in each other's presence. They continued writing letters not because it was novel or simply enjoyable but because both of them sensed that the very formality of the medium was bringing them closer together.

Distance can create closeness, and sometimes it is even the best way to express it. A colleague of mine recently told me about his most memorable image of intimacy in friendship. His mentor had always wanted a cello, and on his sixtieth birthday some of his students chipped in and bought him one as a gift. Years later, my colleague was visiting his mentor, who in the intervening years had also become a friend, at his lakeside cottage. One afternoon, as my colleague emerged from a long swim, he heard the sound of a cello nearby. As he walked up the beach, he could see his mentor, his friend, sitting on a straight chair playing the instrument intently. For a minute my colleague hesitated, but he knew immediately thereafter what he must do. He walked quietly towards his friend, found a chair a good distance away but still within earshot, sat down, and listened. His friend played for a long time, and never before, as he sat distant from him and spoke not a word—never before, he said, had he felt so close to him.

Something like this principle must be implicit in a curious practice among godparents in Spain. Godparents and the parents of the godchild begin using the formal word for "you," *usted,* instead of the familiar *tú* as soon as the godparent-godchild relationship is established. "Compadres become friends and . . . are never stiff with each other but speak with great ease," says Brain (100), but they express that familiarity by indirection.[15]

We can see another example of this principle if we return to those by-now infamous long distance calls I have described. As often as not, my friend and I begin these calls with what would seem to an outsider the most ridiculous and juvenile shouting:

"Hello?"
"Sharp!"
"Ceaser!"
"Sharp!"
"Ceaser!"

Sometimes we go on repeating each other's name for over a minute, pronouncing it now with sweetness, now with shrillness; now with affection, now with a sense of absurdity. This is a complicated dance. Though we have been best of friends for thirty years, we start out calling each other by our last names—a move not unlike the Spanish godparents using *usted.* We do this, I think (though we are not conscious of our motives), because at some level we know that we are reinstituting a formal relationship, and yet we acknowledge the absurdity of such a situation by introducing an element of mockery into our tones. Naming is always ritually charged, and all the more so when the names are repeated, as if to increase the magic. There is clearly a sense in which we are declaring each other's existence, in which we are raising the act of greeting to an almost sacred level and then integrating that greeting into a celebration of our relationship, which we now chant. The repetition of names is more potent than a handshake and less casual than "giving five." It is a kind of verbal embrace that allows us to express affection at the outset without the embarrassment that would inevitably result, at this stage, from a more straightforward expression.

The ritualistic force of exchanging names has its source in the formal ceremonies, still practiced in many cultures, during which friends, as it were, trade names. Jack London, in his story "The Heathen," describes his white western hero exchanging names with Otoo, a native of Bora Bora, and says that "in the South Seas such a ceremony binds two men closer together than blood-brotherhood." Though Charley tells Otoo to stop calling him master, Otoo continues to do so but tells his friend: "'Whenever I think of myself, I shall think of you. Whenever men call me by name, I shall think of you. And beyond the sky and beyond the stars, always and forever, you shall be Otoo to me. Is it well, master?' I hid my smile and answered that it was well" (171–73). The two men wander the seas together for years. One day, having saved his friend from a shark, Otoo is about to lose his own life as a result. As he rises from the water, he calls "Otoo," his own name, which he had exchanged with his friend. "And I could see in his gaze," says Charley, "the love that thrilled in his voice. Then, and only then, at the very last of all our years, he called me by that name. 'Good-by, Otoo!' he called" (196).

"With regard to the exchange of names," says Edward Carpenter, "a slightly different custom prevails among the Bengali coolies. Two youths, or two girls, will exchange two flowers (of the same kind) with each other, in token of perpetual alliance. After that, one speaks of the other as 'my flower,' but never alludes to the other by *name* again—only by some roundabout phrase" (7–8).[16]

Formality can also provide the vehicle for expressions of affection where more direct means fail us. Think, for example, of how much easier it is to tell someone you care for him in a letter than in person. Academics are particularly adept at playing off the formality of inscribing copies of their books or articles for friends. The conventions of inscription sanction the expression not only of gratitude but also of respect and affection. It is not at all uncommon to find either the stuffiest scholar finding his tenderest voice in an inscription or the most laid-back professor rising to rococo elocutionary heights to express his affection for a friend.

The same principle operates in speeches and in dedications of books and poems. Somehow the very formality of the occasion provides one a rare opportunity to express emotion. One sees this in the shy boss who in a speech somehow finds a voice for the fondness he has long felt for his colleague, and one sees it in the laconic gestures of affection that appear as dedications of books. One also sees it in the dedications of contemporary American poetry, where it has become utterly conventional to insert a phrase like "to Marjorie Gillam" or "for Peter and Marie" between the title and the opening line. The dedication is a kind of gift giving in which one offers up one's poem as a part of oneself. This strikes me as a revealing development in a poetry that virtually ignores the subject of friendship. There are exceptions—Lowell, Rich, Piercy, and Merrill most prominent among them—but on the whole, contemporary American poetry has been less willing to take on the subject of friendship than to make some halting gestures on its behalf. The gestures, however, are revealing, for they attempt to summon up the spirit of friendship without actually addressing it or exploring its complexities.

Another device that has become highly conventional in this way is the invocation of a friend's name at a particularly moving point in the poem. For example, in Marge Piercy's "The Homely Wars," a poem that contrasts all-female relationships with male-female relationships, she begins the third section with a direct address to her friend:

Madeline, in your purity I find myself rebuked.
Madeline, in your clarity I find myself restored.

Derek Walcott, in his magnificent poem, "Forest of Europe," dedicated to his friend Joseph Brodsky, turns the invocational convention to advantage by using it to mark a bond that, like the friends' shared sense of exile, is contrasted with their feeling of being outsiders, aliens—Walcott a West Indian and Brodsky a Russian—who haunt the peripheries of the European tradition:

> but now that fever is a fire whose glow
> warms our hands, Joseph, as we grunt like primates
> exchanging gutturals in this winter cave
> of a brown cottage, while in drifts outside
> mastodons force their systems through the snow.

Usually, though, the device is meant to signal an undifferentiated intimacy, which provides a confessional context in which the poet can let his guard down, as Robert Lowell does as early as *Life Studies,* where he refers to his friend's "stuffed duck":

> And there,
> perched on my trunk and typing-table,
> it cooled our universal
> Angst a moment, Delmore.
> ("To Delmore Schwartz")

Lowell uses the technique frequently, as in the ending of his wonderful sonnet for "Randall Jarrell: 1914–1965":

> Randall, the same fall lunges on the windshield,
> the same apples ripen on the whiplash bough.[17]

We also frequently find the direct address in contemporary versions of epistolary poems. In "To Judith, Taking Leave," written in 1962 and dedicated "for J. H.," Adrienne Rich addresses her friend:

> But this little piece of ground,
> Judith! that two women
> in love to the nerves' limit
> with two men—

"Paula Becker to Clara Westhoff," a beautiful later poem by Rich, which contains five direct addresses, ends:

> Clara, I feel so full
> of work, the life I see ahead, and love
> for you, who of all people
> however badly I say this
> will hear all I say and cannot say.

Joseph Brodsky uses the device a number of times in his "Letters to a Roman Friend," most poignantly in these lines:

> Soon, dear Postumus, your friend who loves addition
>   will pay off his debt, his old debt, to subtraction.

Jon Anderson employs this device much less effectively in "A Letter" (which, by the way, is also dedicated "for David Schloss"):

> I put my mouth down in the dark fur, turned
> it over, breathed
>
> Into the warm belly of palm.
> And such repose, David,
> Came over me.

Later in the poem the device appears again:

> And, David,
> but for love of you (& some
> others), I'd give up.

Quoted out of context, the lines seem utterly banal; in context, they are less so, but they remain bathetic nonetheless, for they issue from an isolation that seems more profound than any intimacy that is achieved, or even yearned for. The point of the poem is not so much to celebrate friendship as to show how painful and deceitful the world is by contrast. Friendship, to borrow Anthony Hecht's phrase from his parody of "Dover Beach," becomes "a sort of mournful cosmic last resort" ("The Dover Bitch" 18). Anderson's conception is friendship as support system with a vengeance, and it appears in a book whose title, *Death & Friends,* has nearly as much to say about friendship as the poems in the book, only a few of which address the subject at all. Like the dedication (and like the title of Anderson's book), the convention of invoking a friend's name becomes stale in the hands of an Anderson or a Piercy, but it comes alive in Walcott, Lowell, Rich, and Brodsky. The widespread use of this device reveals a desire to engage the meaning of friendship, and often conveys considerable friendly sentiment; but too often it relies on a vague if sincere gesture of affection as a surrogate for serious consideration of a complex subject.

Although as literary devices the dedication and invocation often seem ineffective in dealing with friendship, as modes of personal address they probably do perform a salutary function. The poet's very willingness to make a public avowal of friendship must itself be a gesture of considerable import for the friend involved and all the more so to the extent that the poet risks sentimentality or makes himself vulnerable, as Anderson does when he says "but for love of you (& some / others), I'd give up."

I have been trying to demonstrate that concealment can be the agent of intimacy, that distance can create closeness, and that formality can provide a vehicle for intimacy. My emphasis has fallen here not because I wish to deny the importance for friendship of openness, closeness, or familiarity, but because we have tended, lately, to lose sight of the formal and to deny its value. And we have done so without realizing the extent to which we have made an ideology of the informal, and consequently, the extent to which the informal has now itself become conventionalized and formalized. We can see this clearly in matters of dress, perhaps most transparently in the homogeneity of the clothes that young people wore in the 1960s as a rebellion against formality and conformity in the mass culture. I have been trying to show how similar conventions operate in our styles and modes of friendship, both in our thinking about it and in our acting out of it. I have been concerned to point up the highly formalistic nature of our relations and to show that, far from shrinking from that recognition, we ought to embrace it. For "in truth," as Wordsworth says, "the prison, unto which we doom / Ourselves, no prison is" ("Nuns Fret Not" 8–9) any more than the sonnet form is a constraint on Wordsworth's—or any other great poet's—freedom. On the contrary, as Wordsworth suggests in this sonnet, form is creativity's way of being free.

A number of people have suggested to me that indirect modes of intimacy are much more characteristic of men's than of women's friendship in western culture. This raises a variety of complex questions, the two most general of which might be worth formulating here: To what extent do the nature and forms of friendship vary along sexual lines? To what extent and in what particular ways is this situation changing, especially as a result of larger changes in the roles of men and women?

There can be no doubt either that friendships do vary along sexual lines or that those variations are themselves now in a state of flux. Indeed, a good deal of recent writing about women has been concerned with just these issues.[18] Sociologists would find fertile ground if they were to explore these areas more fully, for the status and function of friendship in a culture always reflect and influence the nature and structure of other important institutions.[19] My own interest, however, lies in examining the actual forms that friendship does take between men, between women, and between men and women.

In general, I think women do relate more directly and openly than men in contemporary American culture. Even in their manner of greeting friends, women seem to express their affection more directly. Women characteristically hug or kiss; men shake hands or, as in Philip Shultz's novel, they engage in what to an outsider would seem like the most unlikely—to say nothing of unaffectionate—behavior. "I opened my arms," says Raphael when he sees his friend at the door, "and he laughed and dropped the bag and then began the back pounding and punching that's known throughout the western hemisphere as male affection" (61).

The most common arenas for this paradoxically affectionate male slapping and shoving are undoubtedly the playing fields and locker rooms. These are special places where physical contact is sanctioned, but men can also recreate them in their own living rooms. Every time my brother and I see each other (we live in different towns), within the first hour we end up playing a game we played as children, in which we try to push each other over by slapping at each other's hands held at shoulder height. It has become our way of expressing affection through touching, in the face of a still powerful taboo against exactly that. Because it is a game, somehow it feels legitimate. My son must have felt something very much like that legitimacy when he met a new friend a few years ago, had a wonderful time playing with him all afternoon, and ended the day with a spirited wrestling match. A five-year-old American boy would not be caught dead telling a new friend how much he likes him, but not least among the joys of that wrestling match must have been their mutual sense of affection. Boys wrestle because it is fun; they sometimes wrestle with clear intent to do harm; but usually mixed with these motives is the unconscious desire to be affectionate.[20]

To say that women relate more directly than men is not to say that they do not have their own forms of indirection, as *Cranford* clearly illustrates. Exchanging clothes and secrets and a hundred other varieties of gift seems much more prevalent among women and of course these exchanges are highly ritualized and conventionalized activities. Iona and Peter Opie have observed this distinction even on the playground. "Boys," they say, "are definitely realists. The characteristic they most want in a friend is that he should like playing the same games that they do. . . . In girls' friendships, presents and birthday cards, lending things, and sharing sweets" are crucial (323). For every stag party there is a shower; for every poker game there is a sewing circle; for every night out with the boys there is lunch out with the girls. Should exclusively male or female institutions of friendship—fraternities, sororities, clubs, sports, colleges—be promoted or eroded? One woman I know, who would clearly be considered a feminist, told me that she lamented the decline of institutions like tea parties.[21] Stuffy as they were, she said, they provided an occasion to meet and talk—and they did so in a way that allowed enough distance so that one never felt obligated to be confessional. She felt that in many of the recent women's groups the emphasis was mainly on confession and that she often felt compelled to be more intimate than seemed comfortable or advisable. I would add "possible" to her list of adjectives, because here too the pressure to be intimate can as often close as open doors, and when it does open doors, that openness is by no means as free of convention as one might imagine.

Still, men seem to have less recourse than women to direct means of expressing their friendship. Physically, one sees this in the reluctance of American males to hug when they see each other. Though in many countries it has long been standard for men to kiss, only recently have American men begun to hug, and this is still rare enough to make many people, however erroneously, suspect that the relationship may be homosexual. But the awkwardness for men also extends to verbal expressions of affection. Hemingway captures the tone perfectly in *The Sun Also Rises,* where Jake and Bill are about to set off on a fishing trip, which, like boxing and bullfighting, is for Hemingway a highly charged and exclusively male arena of friendship. After a mock argument the hard-boiled, world-weary expatriates suddenly let down their guard:

> "Well," I said. "A plane is sort of like a tricycle. The joystick works the same way."
> "But you don't pedal it."
> "No," I said, "I guess you don't pedal it."
> "Let's lay off that," Bill said.
> "All right. I was just standing up for the tricycle."
> "I think he's a good writer, too," Bill said. "And you're a hell of a good guy. Anybody ever tell you you were a good guy?"
> "I'm not a good guy."
> "Listen. You're a hell of a good guy, and I'm fonder of you than anybody on earth. I couldn't tell you that in New York. It'd mean I was a faggot. That was what the Civil War was about. Abraham Lincoln was a faggot. He was in love with General Grant. So was Jefferson Davis. Lincoln just freed the slaves on a bet. The Dred Scott case was framed by the Anti-Saloon League. Sex explains it all. The Colonel's Lady and Judy O'Grady are Lesbians under their skin."
> He stopped.
> "Want to hear some more?"
> "Shoot," I said.
> "I don't know any more. Tell you some more at lunch."

"Old Bill," I said.
"You bum!" (116)

It is no accident that the issue of homosexuality gets raised here. For one man to tell another, "I'm fonder of you than anybody on earth" would in some places "mean I was a faggot." But notice that as soon as Bill makes this point, he immediately defuses it with humor, as Jake plays along. The words, "Old Bill," then, carry an authentic tenderness, delicately poised as they are against the twin threat of expressing too much and too little affection. Bill completes the subtle harmony by shifting the key and moving into counterpoint: "You bum!" The modulation is brilliant here. Jake and Bill have found a way of expressing their affection which gains strength and significance by confronting and transcending the issue of sexuality.

Just before this exchange takes place, Bill teases Jake about his easy life:

"You're an expatriate. You've lost touch with the soil. You get precious. Fake European standards have ruined you. You drink yourself to death. You become obsessed by sex. You spend all your time talking, not working. You are an expatriate, see? You hang around cafés."

"It sounds like a swell life," I said. "When do I work?"

"You don't work. One group claims women support you. Another group claims you're impotent."

"No," I said. "I just had an accident."

"Never mention that," Bill said. "That's the sort of thing that can't be spoken of. That's what you ought to work up into a mystery. Like Henry's bicycle."

He had been going splendidly, but he stopped. I was afraid he thought he had hurt me with that crack about being impotent. I wanted to start him again (115).

The reference to Jake's sexual obsession and war wound charges the following jokes about homosexuality with a special poignance, but notice that Jake is not worried about his own feelings but about those of Bill: "I was afraid he thought he had hurt me. . . ."

Hemingway is rarely so successful as he is here in portraying affection between men, but this entire exchange gains something of its delicacy and subtle beauty by playing off the taboo against direct male expressions of affection. We ought to lament the taboo and we ought to be encouraged by recent developments that have weakened its hold. But condemning the cause should not prevent us from praising the occasional good effects. There is an analogy here with Jewish humor and the musical form of the blues which came out of Black culture. Both arise from a long tradition of oppression, which should unquestionably be opposed; but our opposition should not prevent us from praising the real achievements and beauties of these forms, both of which gain their identity and strength by turning to account the actual cultural situation of Jews and Blacks. Similarly, our awareness of the limitations of this particular language of friendship should not blind us to the fact that occasionally, as in this example from Hemingway, it can be used with extraordinary creativity and delicacy.[22]

The whole subject of gender differences in friendship deserves far more exploration than I have undertaken here. But it may be more than a routine invocation of the virtues of compromise to suggest that in terms of the issues of form and sincerity, men and women have much to learn from each other. Men must come to see that at some level there is no adequate substitute for self-disclosure, openness, and sincerity, and that in this respect the still dominant male inhibitions are indeed an obstacle to intimacy in friendship. At the same time, women must not glibly pass off male forms of indirection as inevitably at odds with intimacy. Women need to recognize that self-disclosure, openness, and sincerity are not immune to the kinds of conventions and difficulties that we have observed. They are not simple givens; as forms themselves they require no less creativity than any other form.

"One woman I know," says Susan Lee, "said that if as a teenager she had told her parents she'd prefer being with a girl than a boy, they would have sent her to a doctor" (590). "From late childhood onwards," says Brain, "the frank friendships of the playground are not encouraged and are even replaced by a feeling of shame and guilt towards very close friendship which seem to derive from our puritanical attitudes to homosexuality" (24). In his own country, Australia, Brain claims that homosexuality is regarded

> with an out-and-out dread. . . . Swaggering about sexual exploits, dirty jokes, manly manners—all become an attempt to prove you and your mates are as straight as apple pie. Even the physical expression of friendship has been reduced to a strongly ritualistic feinting—as between sparring partners. Australian friends do not hold hands in the street like Trobrianders, caress each other like Bangwa friends, kiss when they meet like Italians, or sleep together like the Nzema, but greet each other with the flamboyant punches and hearty backslapping of professional boxers! (72)

The last part of this description would apply equally to American men, as would both the general fear of homosexuality and its influence on the forms of friendship. But in America I do not think the friendly feelings of childhood are "replaced by a feeling of shame and guilt" so much as by a certain subterranean sense of being on guard against any homoerotic feelings or inclinations. Ironically, increased awareness of homosexuality in our culture inhibits increased physical expression of friendship as often as it enhances it; where tolerance encourages, awareness restrains. In America the more common mode is not to discourage close friendship between members of the same sex but to look upon it suspiciously. We saw this tendency in Bill's joke about how his comment would be interpreted in New York, and we also see it in a wonderful scene in Lillian Hellman's "Julia" in which Sammy Travers remarks casually in a bar that "everybody knew about Julia and [Lillian]," implying that their friendship was homosexual. "I leaned across the table," says Hellman, "slapped Sammy in the face, got up, turned over the table, and went home" (98–99).

Hellman is outraged because Sammy's comment was meant to devalue a relationship that Lillian cherished. A few pages earlier, Hellman is quite candid about the question of homosexuality as she describes spending the night at Julia's grandparents' house one New Year's Eve with Julia when they were twelve years old:

> Very late she turned her head away for sleep, but I said, "More, Julia, please. Do you know more?" And she turned on the light again and recited from Ovid and Catullus, names to me without countries.
>
> I don't know when I stopped listening to look at the lovely face propped against the pillow—the lamp throwing fine lights on the thick dark hair. I cannot say now that I knew or had ever used the words gentle or delicate or strong, but I did think that night that it was the most beautiful face I had ever seen. In later years I never thought about how she looked, although when we were grown other people often said she was a "strange beauty," she "looked like nobody else." . . .
>
> There were many years, almost twenty, between that New Year's Eve and the train moving into Germany. In those years, and the years after Julia's death, I have had plenty of time to think about the love I had for her, too strong and too complicated to be defined as only the sexual yearnings of one girl for another. And yet certainly that was there. I don't know, I never cared, and it is now an aimless guessing game. It doesn't prove much that we never kissed each other; even when I leaned down in a London funeral parlor to kiss the battered face that had been so hideously put back together, it was not the awful scars that worried me: because I had never kissed her I thought perhaps she would not want it and so I touched the face instead. (93–94)

Hellman's tone here is crucial: she acknowledges a sexual element but treats that acknowledgment not as an admission or confession but as a rather obvious and relatively unimportant fact ("I don't know, I never cared, and it is now an aimless guessing game"). What Hellman is opposing here—and what, among other things, she lashed out against when she slapped Sammy Travers—is the kind of crude reductionism that pretends to have come completely to grips with the relationship by, as it were, exposing it as sexual. Hellman knows that her love for Julia was "too strong and too complicated to be defined as only the sexual yearnings of one girl for another." "Certainly that was there," says Hellman, but to have observed its presence is scarcely to have accounted for, explained, or described this extraordinary friendship.

It would be interesting to examine patterns of friendship in homosexual relationships and to compare them with those of both heterosexual relationships and nonsexual same-sex friendships. But the usual way of posing the question of the role of homoeroticism in friendship is not, finally, very interesting or productive. In this respect, little has changed in the twenty-five years since C. S. Lewis felt compelled to undertake "a very tiresome bit of demolition. It has actually become necessary in our time," he said, "to rebut the theory that every firm and serious friendship is really homosexual" (72).[23] There are, clearly, a number of levels at which physical attractiveness influences one's choice of and relations with friends, and there are many erotic spectra across which friends relate. These could be the subject of another book. But simply pointing to the presence of an erotic element in the friendship of two men or two women is like pointing to the presence of competition, aggression, or self-interest. We have no cause to shout "eureka" and believe we have uncovered some fundamental truth or essential animating principle about the friendship.

There are, moreover, other reasons to be wary of placing too much importance on the issue of homosexuality in friendship. The term *homosexuality* covers a multitude of psychic and physical phenomena ranging from passing fantasy to regular practice. The boundaries that separate friendship, love, and sex are always difficult to draw; my own sense is that we learn less about these phenomena if we try to make those lines clear-cut rather than respect their inherent fluidity.[24] We must acknowledge that such conceptual and behavioral territories vary greatly from one culture, and one historical era, to another, and that we tend to map such territories along certain polar axes: normal/abnormal, conventional/unconventional, etc. Whether or not morality enters the picture, we usually want to keep our categories tidy, and anxiety about categorization often skews our vision.

John Boswell tells us that "the erotic content of 'friendship' in antiquity was due in no small measure to the fact that homosexuality was conventional in many ancient societies and could have been part of the relationship; friends of the same sex borrowed from the standard vocabulary of homosexual love to express their feelings in these erotic terms" (135). In the twelfth century, according to Colin Morris, "friends spoke in words which now sound erotic, and lovers not infrequently sound formal and stilted. . . . friendship could be given a more physical expression than in modern Britain; the 'kiss of friendship' would be given in actual fact, and the symbol of the kiss or embrace might therefore express affection rather than sensuality" (96).

Carroll Smith-Rosenberg provides still another example in her extraordinary study of relationships among women in eighteenth- and nineteenth-century America. She describes a world in which "girls routinely slept together, kissed and hugged each other" (22); a world in which women "lived in emotional proximity to each other" (24) as they helped each other through pregnancy, sickness, and death:

> Entire days, even weeks, might be spent almost exclusively with other women. Urban and town women could devote virtually every day to visits, teas, or shopping trips with other women. Rural women developed a pattern of more extended visits that lasted weeks and sometimes months, at times even dislodging husbands from their beds and bedrooms so that dear friends might spend every hour of every day together. When husbands traveled, wives routinely moved in with other women, invited women friends to teas and suppers, sat together sharing and comparing the letters they had received from

other close women friends. Secrets were exchanged and cherished, and the husband's return at times viewed with some ambivalence. (10–11)

These women "frequently began letters to each other with salutations such as 'Dearest,' 'My most beloved,' 'You Darling Girl,' and signed them 'tenderly' or 'to my dear sweet friend, good-bye'" (5n).[25] One letter that Smith-Rosenberg quotes seems (through our eagerly and overly reductive lenses) utterly transparent:

> I wanted so to put my arms round my girl of all the girls in the world and tell her . . . I love her as wives do love their husbands, as *friends* who have taken each other for life—and believe in her as I believe in my God. . . . If I didn't love you do you suppose I'd care about anything or have ridiculous notions and panics and behave like an old fool who ought to know better. I'm going to hang onto your skirts. . . . You can't get away from [my] love. (7)

But for Smith-Rosenberg,

> the essential question is not whether these women had genital contact and can therefore be defined as heterosexual or homosexual. The twentieth century tendency to view human love and sexuality within a dichotomized universe of deviance and normality, genitality and platonic love, is alien to the emotions and the attitudes of the nineteenth century and fundamentally distorts the nature of these women's emotional interaction. . . . There is every indication that these . . . women, their husbands and families—all eminently respectable and socially conservative—considered such love both socially acceptable and fully compatible with heterosexual marriage. Emotionally and cognitively, their heterosocial and their homosocial worlds were complementary. (8)[26]

Smith-Rosenberg concludes from her study that we should

> view sexual and emotional impulses as part of a continuum or spectrum of affect gradations strongly affected

> by cultural norms and arrangements, a continuum influenced in part by observed and thus learned behavior. At one end of the continuum lies committed heterosexuality, at the other uncompromising homosexuality; between a wide latitude of emotions and sexual feelings. (28–29)

Precisely because we are dealing not with a dichotomy but with a continuum—and a very wide continuum at that—it seems to me crucial that we avoid any easy explanations, especially glibly reductive ones, of the relationship between friendship and sexuality.

Just as competition can help each party keep its edge, or self-interest can ironically provide an impetus to goodwill, sexual energy can intensify the mutual attraction of friends. Like competition, aggression, or self-interest, sexuality can also fatally complicate or ruin a friendship, and that is why, I suppose, friendships between a man and a woman become progressively rare as the friendship becomes more intense. Hence the proverb, "When love puts in friendship is gone" (Tilley 399). I do not know whether sexual relations inevitably compromise a friendship, but Nietzsche clearly has a point when he says that "women can enter into friendship with a man perfectly well; but in order to maintain it the aid of a little physical antipathy is perhaps required" (*Human* 297). Joseph Roux, in his *Meditations of a Parish Priest,* asks, "What is love? two souls and one flesh; friendship? two bodies and one soul" (qtd. in Mead 157). Fair enough, but to consider asexuality—or lack of sexuality—as a necessary condition of friendship seems somehow inadequate. And yet mechanisms for protecting male-female friendships from sex are clear. Teenagers, for example, classify such friends as "buddies" or (implicitly distinguishing this category from lovers) *"just* friends." The model is usually familial—"he's like a brother to me"—which means that certain sexual taboos normally associated with kinship relations are in force.[27]

As often as not, of course, these buddy relationships mask rather obvious sexual attractions and provide a secure means of maintaining at least some kind of relationship. Racine's *Berenice* presents the classic situation of the love-friendship conflict. Antiochus, King of Commagene, is in love with Berenice, Queen of Palestine, who considers him her close friend. Antiochus is also the intimate friend of Titus, Emperor of Rome, whom Berenice loves and plans to marry. Near the beginning of the play, Antiochus, on the brink of confessing his love for Berenice, muses alone:

> Long since, she put an end to all my hopes
> And bade me never utter more my love.
> For five years I kept silent; till today
> I hid my passion under friendship's veil.
> (1.2.23–26)

Do Whitman's *Calamus* poems provide a homosexual equivalent to this heterosexual hiding of "passion under friendship's veil"? The issue cuts many ways. Robert Martin points out in *The Homosexual Tradition in American Poetry* that there have been two approaches to this volume of poems. Critics have either acknowledged and condemned the homosexuality or they have denied it and claimed that the poems should be "read as depictions of an ideal, i.e., asexual, friendship." Both approaches, says Martin, proceed from the mistaken "assumption that homosexual content in a work of art invalidates the work" (47–48)—an assumption that Martin's book directly attacks.

The inadequacy of both approaches seems to me clear. To deny homosexuality despite repeated references to men holding hands, kissing, and embracing each other seems ridiculous in itself; but to continue doing so in the face of poems like the following seems utterly unjustifiable:

> Here the frailest leaves of me and yet my strongest lasting,
> Here I shade and hide my thoughts, I myself do not expose them,
> And yet they expose me more than all my other poems.
> ("Here the Frailest Leaves of Me")

One needn't agree with Martin's view that *Calamus* is "a dramatized version of Whitman's acceptance of himself as a homosexual" (52) to see that homosexuality is as dominant in these poems as the taboo against it was in nineteenth-century America. Whitman's recognition of self-exposure occurs simultaneously with his impulse toward concealment, just as, in another poem in this book, his fear of opening up applies to his poetry as well as his actual feelings:

> For an athlete is enamour'd of me, and I of him,
> But toward him there is something fierce and terrible in me eligible to burst forth,
> I dare not tell it in words, not even in these songs.
> ("Earth, My Likeness" ll. 5–7)

The question is not whether or not these poems, to use Martin's phrase, have "homosexual content." Clearly they do.[28] Nor is the question whether that content devalues their quality as works of art. Clearly it does not. The question is whether Martin is right in ignoring the theme of friendship. His solution to the problem of recognizing but condemning homosexuality on the one hand and denying it in preference to asexual friendship on the other is to recognize and praise the homosexuality and treat the theme of friendship as an illusion, at best a merely superficial theme. But must we rescue the poems' homosexual dimensions by denying—or at least ignoring—their concern with friendship? Certainly these poems record experiences and yearnings, ecstasies and anxieties that we see less accurately if we insist on desexualizing them. But there is something narrow and profoundly unlike Whitman about regarding the theme of friendship only as a metaphor for sexuality, even if it does, at one level, serve that function. "I believe the main purport of these States is to found a superb friendship, exalté, previously unknown," says Whitman in "To the East and to the West" (l. 5). Must the desire to legitimize homosexuality force us to read these lines or, say, "For You O Democracy" mainly as a call for gay liberation?

> Come, I will make the continent indissoluble,
> I will make the most splendid race the sun ever shone upon,
> I will make divine magnetic lands,
>   With the love of comrades,
>   With the life-long love of comrades.

I will plant companionship thick as trees along all the
    rivers of America, and along the shores of the great
    lakes, and all over the prairies,
I will make inseparable cities with their arms about each
    other's necks,
> By the love of comrades,
>> By the manly love of comrades.

For you these from me, O Democracy, to serve you ma
    femme!
For you, for you I am trilling these songs.

Whitman's great democratic vision of political unity was of course deeply tied up with his sense of cosmic and artistic unity, all of which he finds implicit in friendship. "I have thought that the invisible root out of which the poetry deepest in, and dearest to, humanity grows, is Friendship," he wrote in 1881 (*Prose* 484). The "new city of Friends" he imagines in *Calamus* is America, which would be transformed by the power of love into "a city invincible to the attacks of the whole of the rest of the earth":

Nothing was greater there than the quality of robust love,
    it led the rest,
It was seen every hour in the actions of the men of that
    city,
And in all their looks and words.
("I Dreamed in a Dream" ll. 3–5)

Is Whitman referring exclusively to sexuality here? I think not. I can find no evidence in *Calamus* to support Martin's claim that these poems suggest "that only when men accept their innate homosexuality can there be any hope for . . . a victory over the aggression, acquisitiveness, and death-drive which, [Whitman] believes, are rooted in heterosexuality" (59). Nor can I agree that the following poem's reference to "the dear love of comrades" refers to homosexuality to the exclusion of friendship:

"I Hear It Was Charged Against Me"

I hear it was charged against me that I sought to destroy institutions,
But really I am neither for nor against institutions,
(What indeed have I in common with them? or what with the destruction of them?)
Only I will establish in the Mannahatta and in every city of these States inland and seaboard,
And in the fields and woods, and above every keel little or large that dents the water,
Without edifices or rules or trustees or any argument,
The institution of the dear love of comrades.[29]

Whitman's democratic vision was rooted in a devotion to equality, which took the form of a passionate embrace of everything from leaf to sky, beggar to president, and cradle to grave. For Whitman, friendship provided the perfect metaphor for his deep sense of connection, acceptance, unity, and cosmic trust. Martin reminds us that Whitman's celebration included homosexual love as well, but if we are to do justice to Whitman's most characteristic quality—his capaciousness—we must resist the tendency to find single-minded impulses. The *Calamus* poems are about homosexuality—and friendship too.

The relation between sexuality and form in friendship can be seen from another perspective if we consider the Nzema of southern Ghana. Nzema men, according to Brain, "'fall in love,' form bond friendships, share their beds, and even marry, but they do not have sex. . . . they make a pact which is accompanied by libations to the ancestors; from then on their love is reinforced by formal and informal rights and obligations" (62). No glib psychoanalytic interpretation of this practice can gainsay the fact that "in most African situations the idea of sex between two men involved in friendship would simply not occur" (63). For the Nzema the act of literally sleeping together implies no more sexuality than does strong handshaking, friendly slapping on the behind, or vigorous backslapping for us. All of these practices—from sleeping together to backslapping—may be sexual displacements, but for our purposes the more important point is that they are also forms for the expression of friendship.[30]

For years now, we have recognized the connections between exotic rituals and high art. But we have not, I think, paid enough attention to the less exotic rituals that surround us every day. The regular poker game, the Monday night gathering for the football game, the monthly lunch date, the morning coffee with the neighbor, the meeting of the regular group at the local pub—these are but some of the residual equivalents, in our culture, to what in more traditional societies are formal institutions for promoting friendship. When we recognize this fact, we begin to find the exotic rituals that I referred to at the beginning of this chapter more familiar and our own practices, one hopes, more endearingly exotic. Among the Chinautleco Indians, for example, who live near Guatemala City, "friendships are made and broken almost with the ceremony and formality of a betrothal between a youth and his fiancée" (Brain 41). In our culture we find such ceremonies mainly among children and adolescents, who also practice various forms of blood brotherhood, an ancient institution that flourished in many cultures long before it reached its ascendancy in pre-Christian Europe.[31] The ritual of exchanging blood, according to Brain, both sanctifies the friendship and endows it with "important supernatural sanctions—having shared each other's blood the couple are considered to have part of each other's essence or being," and the blood also "acts as a magical sanction against the failure of the bonds of friendship" (76–77).

There was no way that this potent ritual could survive the attacks of the Church. After all, blood brotherhood is a kind of "pagan communion between two men rather than a communion with the Christian God" (Brain 81), and as such it had to be squelched by the Church in medieval Europe and colonial Africa. In our culture it survives only in the antics of childhood chums pricking their thumbs and pledging faithfulness. But in Europe and Latin America a new rite replaced blood brotherhood, based on the Catholic practice of co-godparenthood and called by anthropologists *compadrazgo*.

Practiced mainly in Latin America today, though also in parts of Greece, Russia, Spain, Serbia, and Italy, co-godparenthood grew out of the rituals of christening and confirmation, and formalized the tie between the parents of the child and the child's godparents. "The spiritual ties between godparent and godchild were and are secondary" to the friendship bond of the two sets of parents (Brain 95). As with blood pacts, *compadrazgo* both formalized and sanctified friendships, and like blood brotherhood, it eventually came under attack by the Church—this time in the form of Protestant antipathy to ritual. In England these relations were called "god-sibs," but Brain points out that in England "the relationship did not endure as an institution and went through the vicissitudes of social change which the etymology of the word—from godsip to gossip—indicates" (91). Americans may not formalize their godparenthood in church but the institution thrives enough so that to be asked to be the godparent of your friend's child is itself both a powerful declaration and a clear expression of friendship.

To ask a friend to be the godparent of your child is in our culture another example of an art of friendship through indirection. Even if we were to be direct with our friend and say, "we feel so close to you, we'd like you to be Bill's godmother," or "you're such a good friend, we'd like . . ."—even then, the assertion, or rededication, of friendship is formally secondary to the establishment of the godchild-godparent relationship. It is the latter that provides an occasion for the former. And it is that very fact, ironically, that in my view increases the possibilities of intimacy and friendship. All along I have been suggesting that in our culture we have very few social institutions designed explicitly for the preservation and cultivation of adult friendship, and that in the absence of these, we must either capitalize on residual forms, such as the one I have just described, or, say, the institution of the dinner party, or actually create our own forms, as in the case of the long distance telephone game or the shoving matches I have with my brother. The latter especially provide possibilities for creativity that may partially compensate for the problems of communication and uncertainties of expectation that follow from the decline of social institutions and forms for friendship. But once that decline has occurred, as it has in our time, in our culture, we have no choice but to master what forms remain and invent our own. The attempt to circumvent forms in personal relations may not be a great liberation; it may, on the contrary, isolate people more and more the harder they try to relate directly. In naked confrontation, two steps forward often land you three steps backward, as though two magnets, with the best intentions, tried to link up by coming directly at each other.

After his breakdown, John Stuart Mill formed a new conception of happiness as he began to recover: "I never, indeed, wavered in the conviction that happiness is the test of all rules of conduct, and the end of life. But I now thought that this end was only to be attained by not making it the direct end. Those only are happy (I thought) who have their minds fixed on some object other than their own happiness. . . . Aiming thus at something else, they find happiness by the way" (145, 147). The same logic can be profitably applied to friendship. One does derive benefits from friendship, but if they become the object—or even the motive—of the friendship, they evaporate or turn sour. Certainly they are desirable, as are sincerity and intimacy, without which friendship could not exist; but if one pursues any of these directly, they become progressively elusive.

Once sincerity emerges as a central ideology of social relations, as it did in our culture as early as the mid-nineteenth century, the conventions begin to turn on themselves so radically that Emerson could say, "there is no deeper dissembler than the sincerest man" (423). The corollary is put with characteristic hyperbole by Oscar Wilde: "Man is least himself," Wilde says, "when he talks in his own person. Give him a mask and he will tell you the truth" (389). Wilde's epigrammatic pithiness glosses over the equally common problem of hypocrisy, but it seems outrageous precisely because we assume an equation between sincerity and truth on the one hand and masks and deception on the other. Wilde's point is that far from being immune to self-deception, sincerity is even more likely to promote it than role-playing.

As Trilling points out, "authenticity is implicitly a polemical concept, fulfilling its nature by dealing aggressively with received and habitual opinion" (94). That is why I have had to resort to the curious tactic of criticizing sincerity in a book celebrating friendship. I do not mean to devalue its importance any more than Mill meant to denigrate happiness. On the contrary, I want to rescue sincerity from the ideological fog that is its true threat. Sincerity's role in friendship is too important to let it be turned into a pathetic attempt to certify ourselves, which masquerades as a reaching out to others.

Who is it, after all, that relates in a friendship? Thoreau argues that it is not really our deepest selves, in the sense of some central core. "We are poets and fablers and dramatists and novelists ourselves," he says. "We are continually acting a part in a more interesting drama than any written. We are dreaming that our Friends are our *Friends,* and that we are our Friends' *Friends.* Our actual Friends are but distant relations of those to whom we are pledged" (265). Occasionally, says Thoreau, we are lucky enough to have friends treat us as we aspire to be, not as we are. Friends "cherish each other's hopes. They are kind to each other's dreams" (270). "It is the merit and preservation of Friendship, that it takes place on a level higher than the actual characters of the parties would seem to warrant" (271).

If I have been right in insisting that friends invent and play games that can be understood on analogy with works of art, then it will come as no surprise to see Thoreau describing friends as "poets and fablers and dramatists and novelists." It is the indirection of art—its use of form to get closer to reality—that we need to emulate in friendship if we are to recover its infinite possibilities for intimacy, beauty, and meaning. In the next chapter we shall examine the implications for friendship of another form, gift giving, and we shall see that there too it is by indirection that the delicate transactions of gift exchange make their characteristic movement toward both intimacy and spirituality. Like art, gift giving elevates those involved in it to "a level higher than the actual characters of the parties would seem to warrant," and in so doing it provides another hint of a dimension of friendship that can only be called spiritual.

2 Friendship as Gift Exchange

"Give me and I thee and so may we friends be."—Old proverb

There is a stunning moment in Satan's soliloquy in Book IV of *Paradise Lost* in which the doomed hero admits that he is unable to accept God's grace:

> What could be *less* then to *afford* him praise,
> The easiest *recompense,* and *pay* him thanks,
> How *due!* Yet all his good prov'd ill in me,
> And wrought but malice; lifted up so high
> I sdein'd subjection, and thought one step higher
> Would set me highest, and in a moment quit
> The *debt* immense of endless gratitude,
> So burdensome, still *paying,* still to *owe;*
> Forgetful what from him I still *receiv'd,*
> And understood not that a grateful mind
> By *owing owes* not, but still *pays,* at once
> *Indebted* and *discharg'd;* what burden then?
> (4.46–57; emphasis mine)

Satan's problem is that he is unable to accept a gift. He knows that God's love is a gift and he knows that "a grateful mind / By owing owes not," but the weight of God's grace still feels "so burdensome" that he cannot *accept* it. Though rationally he knows better, emotionally Satan sees the gift as creating in him a "*debt* immense of endless gratitude." To be the recipient of infinite love is to be forever in debt.

The language of this passage is economic to the core—a point to which I have called attention by italicizing the relevant words. It is the language of trade, of commodity exchange, of the transactions of the marketplace, and its emphasis on paying and owing stands in stark contrast to the sublime economics of the spirit, which pays no heed to accounts due and debts discharged.

Shakespeare works with a similar complex of issues, though in a more secular context, in the opening of *King Lear,* where the King asks his daughters which one loves him most. After Goneril and Regan shower their father with the flattery he craves, Lear asks Cordelia what she has to say, and she utters her famous response, "Nothing" (1.1.87). Though Cordelia does indeed love her father, she refuses to quantify her love because she knows—as Lear will learn at great cost during the course of the play—that love is by definition not quantifiable. Like Satan, Lear acts as though he were engaged in a business transaction, selling parcels of his kingdom to the highest bidder for his affections. Satan at least recognizes that he is acting out of a fundamental misconception; Lear, on the other hand, pretends to be giving his daughters gifts but in fact wants them to pay.

For Milton the issue is divine love; for Shakespeare, human love. Satan cannot accept a gift, and Lear cannot give one. In both instances—and this is the crucial point—the value of the gift as an ideal is dramatized by following out the consequences of its violation. For Shakespeare and Milton, love is deeply tied up with the notion of the gift.

So too, I want to argue, is friendship. "What friends really mean to each other," says Hofmannsthal, "can be demonstrated better by the exchange of a magic ring or a horn than by psychology" (qtd. in Auden and Kronenberger 200). We need to pause a moment here to consider in some detail the idea of the gift, and I can think of no better way of doing that than to summarize the argument of Lewis Hyde's magnificent recent study of that subject, *The Gift: Imagination and the Erotic Life of Property*. Hyde does not take up the subject of friendship but nearly everything he says in this extraordinary book in one way or another bears on it.[1]

Hyde's fundamental distinction is between gift exchange and commodity exchange. "Scarcity and abundance," he says, "have as much to do with the forms of exchange as with how much material is at hand. Scarcity appears when wealth cannot flow" (*Gift* 22), and since this is usually the case in commodity exchange, there is a link between commodities and scarcity just as there is a link between gifts and abundance: "The gift is a pool or reservoir in which the sentiments of its exchange accumulate so that the more often it is given away, the more feeling it carries, like an heirloom that has been passed down for generations. The gift gets steeped in the fluids of its own passage. . . . What gathers in it is not only the sentiment of generosity but the affirmation of individual good will." ("Food" 56–57)

Another central distinction between commodity and gift is that the former earns a profit whereas the latter gives increase. "The distinction," says Hyde, "lies in what we might call the vector of the increase: in gift exchange it, the increase, stays in motion and follows the object, while in commodity exchange, it stays behind as profit" (*Gift* 37). The gift must always be kept in motion so that "whatever we are given is supposed to be given away again" (*Gift* 4). The gift is like a river and we are its channels, sharing a spirit that is kept alive by its motion.

Not only must the gift be kept in motion; it also "must always be used up, consumed, eaten. *The gift is property that perishes.*" It perishes, that is, "*for the person who gives it away*. In gift exchange the transaction itself consumes the object." Something does often come back after a gift has been given, "but if this were made an explicit condition of the exchange, it wouldn't be a gift" (*Gift* 8–9). Unlike commodity exchange, whose image is the balance of scales, in gift exchange there is always "the sense of imbalance, of shifting weight" (*Gift* 15). The gift is given "with no assurance of anything in return" (*Gift* 9). "Partners in barter talk and talk until they strike a balance, but the gift is given in silence" (*Gift* 15).

Paradoxically, however, "when the gift is used it is not used up. Quite the opposite, in fact: the gift that is not used will be lost, while the one that is passed along remains abundant. . . . What is given away feeds again and again, while what is kept feeds only once and leaves us hungry" (*Gift* 21). In this sense the gift operates in a manner similar to erotic life and the feelings, which "are not used up in use. They may rise and fall, certainly, but they become strong and sure as we use them and only die away when we try to keep the lid on" ("Food" 51).

The dialectic of giving and receiving is central to gift exchange. A commodity, on the other hand, "is truly 'used up' when it is sold because nothing about the exchange assures its return" (*Gift* 23). The curious thing about gift exchange is that it always assumes a return but makes it imperative that that fact not have the status of an expectation. The gift "joins people together. It doesn't just carry feeling, it carries attachment or love" ("Food" 51), and its movement is circular. "The circle is the structural equivalent of the prohibition on discussion. . . . it is as if the gift goes around a corner before it comes back" ("Food" 45).

If commodities move toward profit, gifts move "toward the empty place . . . the gift always moves in its circle from plenty to emptiness. . . . A guest in my home, it has no home of its own but moves on" ("Food" 53–54). The spirit of gift is closely linked with the spirit of hospitality. "There is a force seeking to keep the gift in motion," says Hyde, and that force, which he earlier represents in the image of the river, is the life force itself. The gift's fruits include fertility and growth, and "either the bearers of the gift or the gift itself grows as a result of its circulation" ("Food" 41, 54).[2] The gift is synthetic, not analytic; it "pull[s] things together and lift[s] them up" ("Food" 51). "We spiral upward with the gift, or at least it holds us upright against the forces that split us apart and pull us down" ("Food" 55). Gift exchange is for Hyde profoundly spiritual. It is an economy that takes "the imagination as its model" and is "an emanation of the creative spirit" ("Food" 32).

Hyde admits that "the accumulation of capital has its own benefits—security and material comfort being the most obvious and appealing—but the point here is that whatever those benefits, if they flow from the conversion of gifts to capital then the fruits of the gift are lost. At that point property becomes correctly associated with the suppression of liveliness, fertility, and emotion" ("Food" 60). Hyde also admits that gift exchange itself "has its negative aspects," most important of which is that "the bonds set up by gift exchange limit our freedom of motion. If a young person wants to leave his or her parents, it's best to stop accepting gifts because they will only maintain the parent-child connection. As gifts are associated with being connected to a community, so commodities are associated with both freedom and rootlessness" ("Food" 34).

Hyde's theory of gifts is so laden with implications for friendship that even this brief summary of its central ideas will already, I trust, have suggested some of the essential connections. For gift giving seems to me the quintessential friendly act; indeed, one way of defining the act of friendship may be to say that it is whatever is undertaken in the spirit of gift exchange. My concern is not so much with the actual giving of gifts by one friend to another—though that too is of interest—as with the richness of gift giving as a metaphor for friendship. In adopting this metaphor I assume, with Hyde, the propriety of regarding human relations as exchange.[3] In friendship one exchanges a whole variety of things, from favors to advice, and including one's self, but as we shall see, the very form of exchange (as with the gift) creates a spirit that becomes both the atmosphere in which the exchange takes place and itself the ultimate object of the exchange.

Children, of course, like to give tangible objects as gestures of friendship, and according to Willard W. Hartrup, the practice is even characteristic of human infants and nonhuman primates (14).[4] There is perhaps more continuity than we have recognized between the biblical Jonathan giving David his robe, sword, and bow, and American teenagers giving each other sweaters and "friendship pins" to wear; or blood brothers literally exchanging blood, and Mr. Jones bringing Mr. Smith a bottle of wine. Robert Brain explores the numerous connections between friendship and trade, and suggests that "the efforts which trading partners make to exchange a piece of stone . . . would seem quite out of proportion to the value of the object, or its necessity. Sometimes it seems that a scarcity is almost 'invented' for the purpose of an exchange between self-subsistent peoples in order to keep the peace" (151–52). "Pure commerce, involving profit, is rarely pursued without an injection of altruism and sentiment," says Brain. "Even in a straightforward market relationship, most people prefer to inject an element of friendship" (145, 147).[5]

Though gift exchange is scarcely an exclusively female practice, in our culture women seem to give tangible gifts to their friends more often than men do. "When a woman establishes her relationship with another woman by the giving of gifts," says Louise Bernikow,

> the gifts become metaphors, describe transactions, are in themselves the language of relations. I think of the gifts among myself and the women in my life. . . . At Christmas this year, Nancy gave me a scarf that her sister made and I gave her various body lotions. Leeny made a drawing. I baked bread. Rosemary sent running socks, Vicki a photograph of myself with Honor. There was a poem from one of us to another, a pair of hair combs, a soft purse. . . . What are these things but a laying on of hands? We touch each other through the things we choose to give. We stroke, decorate, adorn and caress one another, both in body and mind. (115)[6]

The relationship between friendship and gifts can also be seen in the proverbial tradition, where one finds dozens of sayings like "With gifts a man may make friends" (qtd. in Whiting 227), or "Little gifts make friend of foe" (qtd. in Whiting 226), or "Small gifts keep friendship alive" (qtd. in Gluski 215).[7] As early as Aristotle, the language of exchange, particularly of gift exchange, seems to be the appropriate language for describing friendship. "The function of a friend," says Aristotle, "is to do good rather than to be treated well" (263), but this applies to friendships of virtue, which Aristotle radically distinguishes from friendships of utility and pleasure. "All men or most," he says, "wish for what is noble, but in fact prefer what is to their material advantage. It is noble to do good to another person without expecting good in return, but it is profitable to be the recipient of good deeds" (241–42). Aristotle is intent on distinguishing the highest friendship from anything that smacks of profit or the marketplace, for the market model of exchange places more value on receiving than on giving. Whereas "most people . . . wish to receive affection rather than to give it . . . the giving of affection seems to constitute the proper virtue of friends" (228–29). Market—or, to use Hyde's term, commodity—exchange is also oppressively attentive to accounting and anxious about whether the scales are balanced. Aristotle associates these "friendships based on usefulness" with "hucksters," and contrasts them with true friendship, which "does not demand what the giver deserves" (225, 244).

Hyde argues that we lose the true spirit of a gift if we give it out of a sense of justice or a self-conscious attempt to restore a balance. Nor can we keep accounts in friendship. "For we do not exercise kindness and generosity," says Cicero, "in order that we may put in a claim for gratitude; we do not make our feelings of affection into a business proposition. No, there is something in our nature that impels us to the open hand and heart" (60).[8] Built into the mechanism of gift exchange is the idea of return: "Give and ye shall receive." But if we give with the intent of receiving, we are investing with the expectation of a future return—and that is not giving at all. If I am generous to my friend because it may later be to my advantage, I am acting out of self-interest, not friendship. As we saw earlier, in the example of *Cranford*, it is perfectly possible for self-interest to coincide with generosity, but if the central motive for the ladies' giving money to Miss Matty had been self-interest, then the gift would not have been an act of friendship.

When you give a gift, says Hyde, "it is as if you give a part of your substance to your gift partner and then wait in silence until he gives you a part of his. You put your self in his hands" (*Gift* 15). The movement is similar in friendship and in both instances the giver makes himself vulnerable. After all, what if there is no return? Many a friend has waited until the silence grows loud with denial or rejection. In friendship, as in gift exchange generally, there must always be an underlying principle of equilibrium. If one friend always does favors for another and there is no reciprocation; if one friend continually brings his troubles to the other but never vice versa; if one friend regularly calls another long distance but it is never the other way around; if one friend is always inviting but never invited—in all of these situations, the friendship obviously will be hard pressed to survive without resentments. On the other hand, if I keep track of how many favors I've done for you and how many you've done for me; if I'm aware that I've listened to your problems three times more this year than you've listened to mine; if I keep a careful accounting of our respective long distance calls, or the number of lunch or racquetball invitations—this accounting too will poison the friendship. The concern with balance cannot intrude itself into the foreground of the friendship without spoiling it, yet without balance, it becomes impossible to preserve the trust that is required for a sustained relationship of giving.[9]

This delicate balance is always difficult to maintain, but when one friend feels betrayed in a friendship, it collapses altogether. For in these terms, betrayal is not equivalent to not giving or returning a gift nor even to not graciously or appreciatively accepting one. It is, rather, like accepting a gift and responding by heaping abuse on the one who gave it. Sometimes simple lack of reciprocity will be experienced as betrayal, but when one believes that one's friend has actively violated the friendship, it is not uncommon for one suddenly to know precisely what the score is. In these circumstances one often not only knows the score—six invitations to three—but one announces it, if not to the betrayer, at least to oneself or to others: "After all I've done for him! After all those favors!" When the gift compact is violated, its magic falls away, throwing one's vulnerability into dramatic relief and thus making one all too ready to revert to the safer mode of commodity exchange.

One way of defining the highest friendships may be to say that they are those in which the issues I have just raised never become problems. In her fascinating study of nineteenth-century American female relations, Carroll Smith-Rosenberg quotes in another context a letter from Jeannie Field Musgrove to her close friend Sarah Butler Wister. "Gratitude," says Jeannie, "is a word I should never use toward you. It is perhaps a misfortune of such intimacy and love that it makes one regard all kindness as a matter of course, as one has always found it, as natural as the embrace in meeting" (4). Montaigne goes even farther, claiming that in true friendship, "services and kindnesses, which keep other [lesser] friendships alive, do not deserve even to be taken into account, by reason of the complete fusion of the wills" of the friends. There is no reason to feel grateful, that is, for doing yourself a service. True friends, he continues, "hate and banish from their thoughts these words that imply separation and difference: benefit, obligation, gratitude, request, thanks, and the like. Everything being in effect common between them . . . they can neither lend nor give one another anything" (99).[10]

By "complete fusion of the wills" Montaigne means more than communal property. True friends for Montaigne virtually share identities—a view that seems to me not only unrealistic but, finally, less idealistic than a view that acknowledges and affirms the separate identities of friends. I say unrealistic simply because it is difficult to imagine such a fusion, and nearly all the other accounts of great friendships—Castor and Pollux, Nisus and Euryalis, Achilles and Patroclus, David and Jonathan, Celia and Rosalind, Hamlet and Horatio, and a dozen others—seem to belie the claim. If Montaigne is right, privacy becomes irrelevant to friendship, a mere vestige of an imperfect relationship. Mary's acknowledgment of Miss Matty's privacy, to take the example of *Cranford,* would be seen as a sign not of their intimacy and mutual respect but of their distance, measured against Montaigne's ideal. But not only does privacy suffer in Montaigne's system; more to the point here, the high idealism of giving would seem trivialized by implication (despite other elements of the essay which celebrate it). In my view, however, the ideal of two separate identities freely giving is considerably loftier than some imagined fusion into perfect unity.

Aristotle acknowledges the importance of balance ("friendships are most durable when each one receives what he gives to the other") but he also understands that in the best friendships "if a person gives more than he receives, he will have no complaints against his friend" (221, 240).[11] Cicero also respects the reality of separate identities, but as with Aristotle, that acknowledgment does not prevent idealism; it enables it. One reason, he says, that good men pursue friendship is "that they may be more inclined to do favors than to receive them: this is the kind of competition—and an honorable kind it is— that will exist between them" (61).

Dr. Johnson's concept of friendship would also find Montaigne's ideal of fusion unrealistic and unattractive, but Johnson goes considerably further than Aristotle and Cicero toward warning of the breaches that can result from excessive generosity. "Benefits which cannot be repaid," says Johnson, "and obligations which cannot be discharged, are not commonly found to increase affection; they excite gratitude . . . but commonly take away that easy freedom, and familiarity of intercourse, without which . . . there cannot be friendship." Johnson is concerned here with acts of generosity having something of the same effect on our friends as God's love of Satan had on him: a feeling of the burden of debt. Being able to accept a gift in the right spirit is sometimes as difficult as being able to give one. "Thus imperfect," says Johnson, "are all earthly blessings; the great effect of friendship is beneficence, yet by the first act of uncommon kindness it is endangered, like plants that bear their fruit and die." Still, Johnson refuses to conclude from this observation that one should not, therefore, be generous to one's friends: "Yet this consideration ought not to restrain bounty, or repress compassion; for duty is to be preferred before convenience, and he that loses part of the pleasures of friendship by his generosity, gains in its place the gratulation of his conscience" (344).[12]

For Dr. Johnson, even if an act of generosity may ironically threaten—or at least strain—a friendship, one has a moral obligation to undertake it. But he shares with Aristotle, Cicero, and Montaigne the conviction that those who seek friendship for advantage (in Cicero's words) "destroy the link . . . that is most productive of affection. It is not so much what we gain from our friend as the very love of the friend itself that gives us joy, and what we get from a friend gives us joy since it comes to us with love" (69). The major source of our joy in friendship lies not in what we receive from our friend but in what we give to him: our love. As with the other advantages of friendship, we do also receive the gifts of our friend, but just as these must not be the motive for establishing the friendship, neither must they be seen as the most important source of joy.

I said earlier that in friendship, as in gift giving, the very form of the exchange creates a spirit that can be seen as both the environment in which the exchange occurs and, ultimately, the most important thing that is exchanged. When Cicero says that "what we get from a friend gives us joy since it comes to us with love," he has in mind a process very similar to the one Hyde describes in which the gift becomes "a pool or reservoir in which the sentiments of its exchange accumulate" ("Food" 56). We tend to think of the friendship itself as the structure in which the exchange occurs rather than the object of exchange, but if we think of the friendship as the spirit that is created when two people relate to each other on the model of gift giving, it becomes clear that friendship is both. Friends do give each other the gifts of their favors, their advice, their concern, their selves, and their souls, but in the best friendships it is the friendship itself that becomes the ultimate gift. For friendship is precisely that pool "in which the sentiments of its exchange accumulate." Like the gift that Hyde says "gets steeped in the fluids of its own passage" ("Food" 56), friendship becomes a kind of presiding spirit in a great friendship, so that, as Hyde says in reference to gifts, "the whole really is greater than the sum of its parts" ("Food" 57). Hyde says that what gathers in the gift is the spirit of generosity and good will, which makes "of those separate parts . . . a band whose wills are focused through the lens of the gift" ("Food" 57). Likewise, I would argue, the generosity and good will that gather in the friendship create a spirituality analogous to what Hyde means when he refers to the whole that is greater than the sum of its parts. "When we have fed the gift with our labor and generosity, it grows and feeds us in return," says Hyde. And the same process occurs when we feed a friendship with our labor and generosity. "The gift and its bearers," according to Hyde, "share a spirit which is kept alive by its motion among them and from that the life emerges, willy-nilly" ("Food" 58).

That is what I mean by the spirit of a friendship, and I believe that it is a creative spirit, as my last chapter argued. For Hyde, who believes that the spirit of gift is also creative, that spirit is closely associated with the mysteriously profound effect of art, and with the paradox that scarcity and abundance are a function of the form of exchange rather than of "how much material is at hand" (*Gift* 22). The gift is associated with abundance because it is essentially creative, but the relationship is deeply paradoxical because the gift cannot be creative without being used up. The gift, we remember, "must always be used up, consumed, eaten. . . . the transaction itself consumes the object." When the gift is used, however, "it is not used up. Quite the opposite, in fact: the gift that is not used will be lost, while the one that is passed along remains abundant" (*Gift* 8–9, 21). In his only reference to friendship, Hyde illustrates this principle with a passage from E. M. Forster's novel *A Passage to India,* in which Dr. Aziz and Fielding have what Hyde calls "a typical debate between gift and commodity" (*Gift* 21):

> "Your emotions never seem in proportion to their objects, Aziz."

"Is emotion a sack of potatoes, so much to the pound, to be measured out? Am I a machine? I shall be told I can use up my emotions by using them, next."

"I should have thought you would. It sounds common sense. You can't eat your cake and have it, even in the world of the spirit."

"If you are right, there is no point in any friendship; it all comes down to give and take, or give and return, which is disgusting, and we had better all leap over this parapet and kill ourselves."

Another way to describe the opposition here would be to understand it as a debate between what Aristotle calls a friendship of utility as opposed to one of virtue. Aziz rejects the commercial model altogether because he knows that an act of friendship cannot be understood as spending and thus depleting some allegedly limited supply (of, say, favors, good will, emotion, or, more generally, friendship itself). It is, rather, an act of giving, in which there is no thought for increasing or decreasing one's own capital—even though, paradoxically, it will lead to increase. We do not use up our friendly emotions by feeling them; on the contrary, we intensify them. "There is nothing more productive of joy," says Cicero, "than the repayment of kindness, or the sharing of interest and exchange of favors" (68). By spending good feeling, we don't decrease our supply; we increase it.

Hyde makes this point by contradicting Fielding directly: "In the world of gift . . . you not only can have your cake and eat it too, you can't have your cake *unless* you eat it" (*Gift* 21). A perfect illustration of the applicability of this principle to friendship can be seen in *Cranford*. In response to Miss Matty's financial troubles, her maid Martha decides to make a pudding for dinner with her own money because she knows Matty can no longer afford her favorite dish. Martha goes "to an old teapot in which her private store of money was deposited" and takes out enough to buy the ingredients (184). After lovingly preparing the pudding, she brings it in to Matty, who is so moved that she tells Martha, "I should like to keep this pudding under a glass shade, my dear" (187).

Matty's instinct is perfectly comprehensible: she wants to preserve this embodiment of friendship. But for the narrator, who was also at the dinner,

> the notion of the lion *couchant* [which was the shape of the pudding], with his currant eyes, being hoisted up to the place of honour on a mantelpiece, tickled my hysterical fancy, and I began to laugh, which rather surprised Miss Matty.
> "I am sure, dear, I have seen uglier things under a glass shade before now," said she.
> So had I, many a time and oft; and I accordingly composed my countenance (and now I could hardly keep from crying), and we both fell to upon the pudding, which was indeed excellent—only every morsel seemed to choke us, our hearts were so full. (187)

The mixture of tears and laughter here is perfectly appropriate, but the key point is that they all know, finally, that the only way to accept the gift is to consume it—and that that too, paradoxically, is the only way to preserve it.[13]

The principle of consuming to preserve, or spending to make abundant, raises interesting questions about the number of friendships one can have at any one time. Is there, in other words, a more traditional principle of limitation in this regard even if within a given relationship a paradoxical principle of abundance and scarcity operates? The classical tradition takes the view of moderation. Plutarch, for example, warns of the conflicting demands on one's time and loyalty from different friends (*Many Friends* 57–59) and Aristotle says directly that "intimate friendship is only possible with a few people" (268). It is Montaigne who enforces the strictest economies:

> Common friendships are divisible; one may love one person for his beauty, another for his ease of manner, another for his liberality, this one for his paternal affection, and that one for his brotherly love, and so on. But that friendship which possesses the soul and rules over it with complete sovereignty cannot possibly be divided in two.

If two called on you for help at the same time, to which of them would you run? If they asked contradictory services of you, how would you reconcile them? If one of them told you a secret which it would be useful for the other to know, how would you get out of the quandary? A unique and dominant friendship dissolves all other obligations. The secret that I have sworn to reveal to no other, I may without perjury communicate to him who is not another—but is myself. (100–101)

Whatever pragmatic arguments Montaigne advances in support of his position, the most important consideration for him is that in a perfect friendship "each gives himself so absolutely to his friend that he has nothing to dispose of elsewhere" (100). But if Hyde is right about the gift's creative powers, then Montaigne's concept seems constricting. For if one truly gives oneself absolutely to a friend, it does not follow that there will be nothing left; on the contrary, there will be more than there was before one gave. But one's supply of energy or time is not endless, and there clearly is a sense in which the best kinds of enthusiastic giving use up even more energy than less intense acts of friendship. It is precisely because one does not have an inexhaustible store of energy or time that one's choice of friends becomes so important; in this sense, scarcity seems directly related to value. There must be limits to the number of friendships one can maintain at any given time. The difficulties of sustaining numerous friendships cannot be underestimated but they stem from these kinds of pragmatic matters, which Plutarch and Montaigne also raise, not from the commodity exchange model of inherent limitations of feeling that Montaigne relies on here.

Earlier in his famous essay Montaigne seems to assume a position closer to Hyde's. Contrasting friendship with sexual love, where "there is only a frantic desire for what eludes us," Montaigne says that "friendship is enjoyed even as it is desired; *it is bred, nourished, and increased only by enjoyment,* since it is a spiritual thing and the soul is purified by its practice" (94, emphasis mine). One might say that for Montaigne, Hyde's principle of abundance applies at a micro level.

Montaigne is primarily concerned with one intense bipartite relationship, while Hyde is mainly concerned with group relations. Indeed, Hyde is careful to make this distinction. "Reciprocal giving," he says, "is a form of gift exchange, but it is the simplest. The gift moves in a circle and two people do not make much of a circle. . . . The smaller the circle is—and particularly if it involves just two people—the more a man can keep his eye on things and the more likely it is that he will start to think like a salesman. . . . When the gift moves in a circle its motion is beyond the control of the personal ego, and so each bearer must be a part of the group and each donation is an act of social faith" (*Gift* 16).

Notice that Hyde does not deny that gift exchange—in his full sense—can take place between two people; he only claims that a two-way exchange is the simplest form of it, and he suggests that it is the most difficult to sustain because the corner that the gift must turn before coming back is always visible to both parties. I take this point not as a suggestion that gift exchange provides an inadequate model for friendship but rather as an indication—and partly an explanation—of the difficulty of friendship. Keeping score is considerably easier when you and I are the only participants in the exchange than it is when, as in the classic case of the Massim tribes near New Guinea, thousands of people scattered over a dozen groups of islands are involved in the Kula, the ceremonial gift exchange of armshells and necklaces.

What is so remarkable about the Kula, and what Hyde sees as typical of gift exchange, is the extraordinary power of indirection (*Gift* 12–16). You give freely, you wait in silence, and something is given to you. Dramatic illustrations of this principle as it applies to friendship will be considered when we take up *The Merchant of Venice* in the next chapter, but the point can also be seen in the climactic episode of Lillian Hellman's "Julia." Lillian has agreed to be the courier for fifty thousand dollars, which her friend Julia wants to get to Germany in 1937 to secure the release of political prisoners there. "We think all will go well," she is told, "but much could go wrong" (87). At great risk Lillian boards the train for Berlin. "Before I reached my coach, a young man was standing holding a valise and packages. He said, 'I am W. Franz. . . . This is a birthday present from Miss Julia.' He handed me a box of candy and a hatbox . . ." (90). The hatbox, of course, contains the money, and it has a note attached to it, which says, "There is no thanks for what you will do for them. No thanks from me either. But there is the love I have for you. Julia" (91).

The fact that the pretext is a gift is crucial, for what Julia is giving her friend is the opportunity to give. The elaborate indirection that Lillian must follow to complete the financial exchange successfully also holds for the subtle gift exchange that is being transacted here. Julia's gift to her friend must be indirect. Had her motive been to provide an occasion for Lillian to give, Julia could not have given the gift. Only by pursuing another object—saving lives—could she find the indirect means to give a gift simultaneously to her friend. In this connection it will be useful to recall the point I made about indirection in my last chapter, where I argued that forms provide just such indirection as is needed to foster and express intimacy in friendship.

Julia's statement that there is no thanks either from her or from the people who will be freed from prison is meant to establish this exchange as one of gift and not commodity. The brutal irony is that the ghastly conditions in Nazi Germany—in which (to continue the economic metaphor) human lives have become cheap—have made it necessary to resort to buying lives, as it were, through bribery. The stakes are high but Julia can promise no tit for tat, no straightforward return on Lillian's risk. It is as though Julia sees herself as part of a much larger circle whose very preservation is at stake in such a way as to require great individual sacrifice. That circle is symbolically related to the circle in which the gift moves. When Lillian arrives in Berlin and meets her connections, the same pretext is used in order to hand over the packages. "I am so glad to see you again," she says to them. "I have brought you a small gift, gifts" (111). They take the packages and disappear.

By thus keeping the gift moving, Lillian has successfully accepted Julia's gift. When they meet again, Julia tells her "it is my money you brought in and we can save five hundred, and maybe, if we can bargain right, a thousand people with it. So believe that you have been better than a good friend to me, you have done something important" (113). The two friends have given to each other, but unself-consciously, and only in so doing have they been able to give to others as well.

Julia's understanding of the relation between gifts and friendship does not go unnoticed by Lillian. Julia had become an ardent socialist, "and lived by it," says Lillian, "in a one-room apartment in a slum district of Vienna, sharing her great fortune with whoever needed it. She allowed herself very little, wanted very little. Oddly, gifts to me did not come into the denial: they were many and extravagant," including a Toulouse-Lautrec drawing, expensive jewelry, clothes, and furniture (88). Julia's socialistic economics did not, clearly, prevent her from understanding another economics. Together, Lillian and Julia prove the paradoxical logic of what Hyde calls the "economy of the imagination" ("Food" 32), for in gift exchange costs increase gains. What friends give each other does not move out of circulation (as in commodity exchange) but increases the value of the friendship itself.

A similar example of a friend's gift being the opportunity or means to give is provided in Montaigne's story of Eudamidas:

> Eudamidas of Corinth had two friends, Charixenus of Sicyon and Aretheus of Corinth. Being a poor man, and his two friends being rich, when he came to die he made his will in this form: "To Aretheus I leave the task of supporting my mother and providing for her old age, and to Charixenus the duty of finding a husband for my daughter and giving her the biggest dowry he can afford; and in case either of them should die I appoint the survivor to take his place." The first to see this will laughed at it, but when the heirs were notified they accepted it with extreme satisfaction. And when one of them, Charixenus, died five days later and the succession fell on Aretheus, he took scrupulous care of the mother and, out of his estate of five talents, gave two and a half

as a dowry to his only daughter and two and a half to the daughter of Eudamidas, celebrating both their weddings on the same day. (100)

Our initial reaction to this tale is to admire the loyalty of Aretheus and to see it as a high act of friendship. Montaigne agrees but he believes that "beyond all doubt, the power of friendship is much more richly displayed in the terms of [Eudamidas's] will than in Aretheus's actions" (101). Montaigne would also regard Julia's act of friendship as greater than Lillian's, for there too one friend gave the other the means of giving a gift. "Eudamidas bestows on his friends," says Montaigne, "the grace and favour of employing them in his need. He makes them heirs of his own liberality by thus putting into their hands the means of benefiting him" (101). For Montaigne and Hellman alike, giving—to borrow the words of Gavriel in Elie Wiesel's *The Gates of the Forest*—"is a privilege which has to be earned" (15). Though I suggested earlier that Montaigne's ideal of perfect unity implies problems for the ideal of gift exchange, it seems clear that in this story he takes the idea of gift exchange very seriously indeed, though even here the theme of communal property is present. For Montaigne provides this anecdote as an illustration of one of the philosopher Diogenes' dicta. When Diogenes "had need of money," says Montaigne, "he used to say that he asked it *back* from his friends, not that he asked them for it" (100).

In the last chapter I explored the principle of indirection in terms of form and its relation to intimacy and authenticity. In this chapter I have been examining the same principle in the context of the gift. I should now like to explore some of the connections among these contexts by examining the structure of Cicero's essay on friendship and demonstrating that it is informed by this same fundamental principle of indirection.

Cicero's *On Friendship* is presented mainly as a dialogue between Laelius, the main speaker, and Fannius and Scaevola, who ask the questions and offer their responses, but clearly play a subordinate role. The essay does not begin with the dialogue; it begins, instead, with a kind of letter or address from Cicero to his friend Atticus. In this address Cicero acknowledges that Atticus has often asked him to "write an essay on friendship, and I quite agree," he says, "that it is a subject that everyone ought to think about, and that it is particularly deserving of the consideration of men who have been as close friends as you and I" (46). Cicero's procedure for writing that essay, he says, will be to record a discussion of the subject between Laelius, Fannius, and Scaevola, which took place after the death of Laelius's close friend Scipio. But Cicero was not present at that discussion; he heard about it from Scaevola, who happened to be a friend of his too, and who related the story on an "occasion when he was sitting on a bench in his garden . . . in the company of a few close friends, I among them" (45).

If this sounds complicated, it is. I have tried to simplify the complexities, but we are still left with a remarkably complicated narrative frame: *On Friendship* is an address to Cicero's friend in which he records a dialogue that took place between some friends of another friend, and which that other friend reported to him. We have a story within a story within a story—a narrative device that, although not unconventional, was certainly not the only form open to Cicero. Why, then, we must ask, does Cicero choose this form for his essay?

The answer, I think, lies in what we can only call a principle of immortality. The friendship of Laelius and Scipio was legendary in Rome. Laelius says he hopes "that for all time to come men will remember my friendship with Scipio. And I cherish this hope the more because in all the course of history men can name scarcely three or four pairs of friends; to this category, I venture to hope, men will assign the friendship of Scipio and Laelius" (52). This conventional classical concept of immortality through art and legend may seem more congenial to our secular age than do those religious concepts of immortality associated with one or another version of heaven. In the same context of friendship we have a familiar example from *Hamlet,* where the dying hero implores Horatio not to follow him to death:

> If thou didst ever hold me in thy heart,
> Absent thee from felicity awhile,
> And in this harsh world draw thy breath in pain
> To tell my story.
> (5.2.351–54)[14]

Laelius is blunt about his view. "As far as I am concerned," he says, "although Scipio was taken away from me unexpectedly, he is still living and will live forever, for it was the man's virtue that I loved, and this has not been destroyed" (89). By using the death of a friend as the occasion for reflecting on friendship, Cicero inaugurates a tradition that goes on to include St. Augustine's remarks on friendship in his *Confessions,* Montaigne's meditation on La Boétie, a long line of pastoral elegies both before and after Milton's "Lycidas," and modern works as diverse as Solzhenitsyn's *The Oak and the Calf,* John Knowles's *A Separate Peace,* Toni Morrison's *Sula,* Fred Uhlman's *Reunion,* and Lillian Hellman's "Julia."

We begin to see the direction in which Cicero is moving when he remarks, in his prefatory address to his friend Atticus: "It is a fact that discourses of this kind, when placed in the mouths of men of an earlier day—especially if they be men of distinction—carry with them, somehow, a greater degree of conviction. Yes, indeed! Sometimes, when I am reading what I myself wrote, I get the strange feeling that it is actually Cato, and not I, who is doing the talking!" (46–47).

Cato is the character who, in Cicero's related essay "On Old Age," plays a role analogous to Laelius's in "On Friendship." There is a sense, Cicero suggests, in which these men really are still alive—a sense that is closely connected with what we mean when we speak of a "living tradition." I want to suggest that a useful way of understanding the sense in which Laelius or Scipio is still alive is to consider the analogy of the gift. Laelius claims that it is Scipio's virtue that lives on. If we take virtue to represent Scipio's gift, then the gift lives on because it has been kept in motion. And it has been kept in motion first by Laelius, who spread the word to Scaevola, then by Scaevola, who passed it on to Cicero, and now by Cicero, who passed it on to Atticus. In every case we have a friend passing along a gift to another friend. Nor is it straining to suggest that by the time we get to Cicero's injunction to Atticus ("read it, and you will recognize yourself" [47]), we are meant to see this as a generalized address to all readers of the essay. Not only has Cicero just said that friendship "is a subject that everyone ought to think about" (46), but his tone throughout is remarkably personal and intimate. He—and Laelius who speaks for him—adopts a tone perfectly suited to an essay on friendship.

By speaking in this way, Cicero casts his reader in the role of a friend (Atticus is our stand-in) and thus implicates us in the magic circle of the gift. Cicero thus fulfills Laelius's desire for immortality by passing his gift down through the ages. Hyde tells us that his own "experience of poetry (both of reading and writing) had been in the nature of a gift: something had come to me unbidden, had altered my life, and left me with a sense of gratitude," which he defines as "a labor the soul undertakes to effect the transformation after a gift has been received" ("Food" 32–33).

We might generalize the point to all art, even to our experience with great ideas, teachers, minds, spirits. It may seem odd to think of our response to art or ideas in terms of gratitude, and yet clearly we do often feel that we have been given a gift, that our lives have been (as we say, in our significantly economic language) "enriched" by hearing a Dickinson poem or a Beethoven symphony, by seeing a Rembrandt, by reading *The Republic,* or by coming under the influence of a great teacher. Perhaps the connection between gratitude, in this sense, and what I have been calling immortality will become clearer in the light of the following anecdote.

A few years ago, when I was planning the revival of *The Kenyon Review,* Robert Hass—whose poems we had just accepted for the first issue—told me about a manuscript that he had recently received "out of the blue." Consisting of some chapters of a book in progress, it had simply arrived in Hass's mail one day. He knew nothing about the author but he found the work so extraordinary that he wanted to recommend it to me. Hass sent along the chapters, I too found them extraordinary, and in two installments we soon published them in the new *Kenyon Review.*

About the same time that I originally wrote Hass, my co-editor showed me another manuscript. This was a forthcoming book called *Number Our Days* by the anthropologist Barbara Myerhoff. The book was based on Barbara's fieldwork at a Jewish community center near Los Angeles, where she was studying the relationship between ethnicity and old age. A Jew herself, but secularized, Myerhoff had written a number of ethnographic studies of exotic cultures, but during her experience with these elderly men and women who had long ago been displaced from a hundred Eastern European *stetls,* she came to discover that her own culture was to her the most exotic and fascinating of all.

Number Our Days is a curious blend of anthropological analysis, oral history, personal essay, and novelistic narrative. It is all of these forms and yet it is also something of an autobiography and a confession, whose origin can be traced to Augustine's *Confessions* and especially to Wordsworth's *Prelude,* works that record the growth of a personal vision and its emergence into lucidity. Myerhoff's discovery of her own culture and her own cultural identity never obtrudes itself into the foreground of her narrative, which is reserved for the brave, compassionate, swaggering, petty, and wise characters who populate the community center and the book with the bittersweet stench of profoundly imagined reality.

It had been a long time since a single book had spoken to me so intimately and profoundly of my own experience. I called Myerhoff the next day and asked if I could go through the manuscript and cut and paste together a twenty-five-page essay for *The Kenyon Review.* She agreed.

The task was sweet torture: how to pick and choose from all that treasure and still come up with a coherent freestanding essay. By the end of the next week I felt as though I had assembled a puzzle with 10,000 pieces—or rather that I had designed and assembled such a puzzle, according to a pattern that Barbara had already created but that I could only discover, as it were, by recreating it. The first step in that direction had been my initial reading. My job as editor was to shape, with the assistance of my coeditor, an essay that would make it possible for readers of *The Kenyon Review* to experience something of what I had, but in five percent of the space.

When Barbara received the draft of what I had done, she called to tell me that "something strange is going on here. You've selected every one of my favorite parts of the book. Not just a few but every damn one."

The essay appeared under the title "A Renewal of the Word" in our first issue, and the response was overwhelming; nothing we have published since has generated such a flood of positive mail. A few months later I was notified that "A Renewal of the Word" would be reprinted in the Pushcart anthology and that it had won the Lamport Award, which is given annually to the single best essay published in an American magazine. When I called Barbara to tell her the good news, we discovered that, though she was ten years older than I, we grew up in virtually the same neighborhood and had both spent half our childhoods eating hamburgers with grilled onions at Mawby's Grill in Cleveland.

A few days later Barbara wrote to say she had decided to give the prize money to the widow of Shmuel, the poet-philosopher-tailor who had been the focus of the piece we had published and who had died shortly after the release of the film Barbara had made a few years before about the same people (a film that won an Academy Award). Barbara asked if I would please write Rebekah a note telling her something about the response to the essay and about my own response to Shmuel.

Barbara's letter arrived on one of those days when the manuscripts were overflowing my desk, my copyeditor was demanding that I finish reading proofs for our next issue, the phone was ringing off the hook, meetings were scheduled all afternoon, and the ever-mounting stack of unanswered mail was beginning to threaten my threshold of tolerance. I loved Barbara's book, I loved the essay, I loved Shmuel, and I think I loved Rebekah too. But I was busy; never had I had more work to do, and since Barbara asked that I write to Rebekah as soon as possible, I decided to fire off a quick missive and be done with it. I was not resentful, just busy. And so by evening my quick note was on its way to Rebekah while I nursed more than a little guilt for not taking more time and care with the matter.

But the guilt didn't last long. It got buried beneath more urgent imperatives and the daily press of work. So six months later it came as a pleasant surprise to receive a phone call one afternoon from Barbara. She had just finished writing the afterword for the paperback edition of her book and wanted to read it to me. "Between Rosh Hashana and Yom Kippur," she began, "I arranged to present Shmuel's widow, Rebekah, with 'The Pushcart Prize.' . . . I wanted Rebekah, and Shmuel, to receive the honor in some public manner, among their own people. I knew this was somewhat risky in view of Shmuel's controversial politics, but ultimately worth it, it seemed to me." I listened patiently as Barbara read on:

> My presentation was incorporated into the Oneg Shabbat which was particularly well-attended because of the holiday. Apples and honey were served. The mood of reconciliation called for by the season suggested itself as people greeted one another, *Shanah tovah tikkatevu* . . . "May you be inscribed in the Book for a sweet year." Still, Rebekah was nervous and so was I. I began by describing the prize, the recognition it carried and then mentioned Shmuel's name. Several people grumbled audibly. One woman actually left the hall and others made gestures or sounds of disgust. Rebekah stood beside me trembling but maintained her poise. Over the din I began loudly to read from a letter of congratulations to Rebekah written by Professor Ronald Sharp, one of the editors who had nominated Shmuel's piece for the prize. "Shmuel articulated a sensibility and a sense of the world that illuminated my own life . . . His brave dignity, his piercing and wide-ranging intellect were refined, not diluted, by his tenderness and deep sense of fragility . . . I think of Shmuel as one of the greatest characters I have encountered in a lifetime of reading. He stands, for me, with the great heroes. You and Shmuel gave Barbara the highest gift one can give . . . In her book she kept

the gift moving, as all true gifts must be. The gift still moves. It has been passed to me and I have passed it on to many others. You and Shmuel have a continuing life that, for all of us, is pure gift. Thank you."

The hall was suddenly still. Rebekah took the letter, the book, the money and stepped up to the microphone. "I wanted to read in Jewish for you from Shmuel's poems," she said. "But I no longer read aloud since my accident." She pointed to her mouth. On April Fool's Day, Rebekah had been running to catch a bus. Two boys stretched a rope across the sidewalk before her. The fall had knocked out all the upper teeth in half her mouth. "So I will say only this," she continued. "It is a good thing for a person to get this attention because otherwise you could come to doubt that you see things the way they really are. All my life with Shmuel I enjoyed immensely his outlook and his mind and learning. He was my teacher, my best friend and my lover. 'My beloved is gone down into his garden, to the beds of spices, to feed in the gardens, and to gather lilies. He is altogether lovely. This is my beloved and this is my friend, O Daughters of Jerusalem.'"

In the complete silence that lasted until Rebekah sat down, some of the women could be heard weeping. A couple of women walked across the hall to embrace Rebekah. The moment was so tender as to be unfamiliar in this place. Truly these were Days of Turning. (*Number* 275–76)

My words came back to me as in a foreign tongue, as though they had a strange author and came from another time and place. And yet they were more familiar to me than the sound of my own weeping, which now came in great joyous sobs over that long distance line from Los Angeles to tiny Gambier. Later, as I thought about this rare conversation and the surplus of emotion that I had felt, I realized that it was Lewis Hyde's theory of gift exchange—from which I had drawn in my letter to Rebekah—that provided the best explanation of what had happened. For Hyde had shown that a true gift is always kept moving and that its very movement increases its value. One loses the spirit of a gift if one gives it with the intention of paying back a debt or balancing an account. Had I attempted to write a letter to Rebekah that would heal the breach in her community, it obviously would have been a failure. What had happened, instead, was that in the press of daily circumstance I had simply tried to tell Rebekah how important Shmuel and Barbara's book had been to me. Only later did I realize that among the many powerful emotions I experienced upon reading *Number Our Days* was gratitude in the sense I have already described: gratitude to Barbara, to Shmuel, and to all the others. Barbara and Shmuel had given me an extraordinary gift. Had I somehow set out to pay Shmuel back, as though I were discharging a debt, I never could have given him a gift. This, as I suggested earlier, is Satan's problem in *Paradise Lost*. So great is his sense of obligation, of having to repay God for what he has been given, that he is unable to accept God's grace, which is by definition given freely. It was only through indirection—that is, writing a note of thanks to Rebekah, and such a casual and hasty one at that—that I was able to give a gift to Shmuel in return.

What is worth noting here is the relationship between this kind of indirection, the indirection whereby (as I suggested in my last chapter) intimacy can often be best expressed by highly formal means (both in art[15] and in friendship), and the kind of reflexivity that was so central to that telephone conversation between Barbara and me. For in that conversation, she read to me from an afterword she had written for a new edition of her book. In that afterword she described not simply my letter but her reading of my letter to the audience. As with Cicero's tale within a tale within a tale, the structure here consisted of embedded narratives. And again, as with Cicero, a gift was being passed along in each renewal of the word. Never did I understand more clearly what Laelius meant when he said that Scipio "is still living and will live forever"—or what Cicero meant when he said that he sometimes gets "the strange feeling that it is actually Cato, and not I, who is doing the talking!" For surely there is nothing mystical in observing that Shmuel's spirit was indeed still alive, that he had successfully turned his own life into a gift and passed it along; and that in some sense by keeping the gift moving Barbara and I had found ourselves enfolded in a circle whose power and magic Hyde attempts to describe and whose vital presence one can only hint at with words like "immortality." When the gift is kept in motion, the universe becomes a familiar place, an answering place, a more intimate home; it feels like a living tissue of coincidence, a seamless web of purposeful accident. It becomes, that is to say, a friendly place.

A few months after the call from Barbara, I was still trying to make sense of these events. I found myself talking about them obsessively, continually trying out new formulations. One afternoon in San Francisco I went on in earnest for an hour; suddenly everything started making sense, and I began to form an explanation very much like the one I have just provided. The man who was sitting across from me, listening patiently to my furious attempt to articulate a coherent view, was Robert Hass, who about a year before had sent me that manuscript I referred to earlier. As I gestured and gesticulated he finally broke out in the smile that I had seen him politely trying to repress for half an hour, and as soon as the smile was out I remembered as if on signal that the manuscript Bob had recommended was Lewis Hyde's study of gift exchange. "I agree, I agree," said Hass, and then, with consummate grace: "Didn't you mention this guy Hyde to me once before?"

In an age that has been exceptionally attuned to lapses into sentimentality, one probably ought to be more reluctant than I have been to appropriate the metaphor of gift giving to friendship—and all the more so when that model carries with it such heavy spiritual freight. It is, after all, a long way down from Cicero's claim that "of all the gifts the gods have given us, [friendship] is our best source of goodness and happiness" (67) to Richard Nixon's birthday greeting to John Mitchell in 1979, when he presented him with a gold watch. "Friendship," Nixon inscribed on the watch—probably imagining he was composing the lines on the spot—"is a gift of the gods and a most precious boon to man."[16]

There are, to be sure, more cynical ways of conceiving friendship as a form of exchange. Montesquieu, for example, said that "friendship is a compact by which we undertake to do someone small favors in expectation of receiving big favors" (qtd. in Guterman 178–79). And La Rochefoucauld, perhaps the most famous cynic about friendship, said that "what men call friendship is really only a society, a reciprocal servicing of interests, an exchange of good offices; it is finally only a commerce, in which *amour-propre* proposes to itself something to be gained" (qtd. in Keohane 292).[17]

The classical ideal of selfless friendship has always been a sitting duck for satire, and at least since the Renaissance it has been customary to question whether the great ancient accounts of friendship are not so idealized as to present an unrealistic picture of the frail human relationship we have all known friendship to be. In this regard, Montaigne's fine essay seems perhaps the most vulnerable of all. When we turn to meditations on friendship, do we want a description of the light that never was—or which burns brightly perhaps once in a hundred years—or do we want an anatomy of the more familiar flicker?

I tried to address this issue in my last chapter by arguing that the presence in a friendship of aggression, competition, or self-interest does not in itself compromise the relationship. I also suggested that reductionism is at least as serious an obstacle to our intelligent reflection about friendship as any of the many versions of sentimentality. But as for the matter of spirituality, no serious examination of friendship in our time can ignore the extent to which friendship has assumed that status.

Not that this is a recent development. On the contrary, friendship has a deep spiritual association in both the biblical and the classical traditions. "A faithful friend is the medicine of life," says Ecclesiasticus (6:16), and in John 15:13 we read: "Greater love hath no man than this, that a man lay down his life for his friends." This spirit of sacrifice finds a biblical parallel in the story of David and Jonathan, and a classical parallel in the legend of Damon and Pythias. Condemned to death for plotting against Dionysius I of Syracuse,

Pythias was granted leave to return home to arrange his affairs after Damon gave himself up as a pledge for his friend's return. At the last minute Pythias did return and the tyrant, impressed by the courage of both, remitted the sentence and asked to be friends himself with Damon and Pythias. "Such indeed are the powers of friendship," concludes Valerius Maximus (c. 49 BC to c. AD 30) in his rendering of the tale: "to breed contempt of death, to overcome the sweet desire of life, to humanize cruelty . . . to which powers almost as much veneration is due as to the cult of the immortal gods. For if with these rests the public safety, on those private happiness depend; and as the temples are the sacred domiciles of these, so of those are the loyal hearts of men as it were the shrines consecrated by some holy spirit" (Selden 174).

The associations between friendship and spirituality in the Judeo-Christian tradition are so numerous as to make an appropriate subject for a book. Adele M. Fiske has written one on a single element of that tradition: *Friends and Friendship in the Monastic Tradition.* For Saint Bernard, Anselm, and Aelred, friendship was, as Colin Morris has argued, "the paradigm of the whole Christian life" (106). The views of Aelred, abbot of Rievaulx in England, advisor to Henry II, and author of a remarkable treatise called *Spiritual Friendship,* were extraordinarily popular in the twelfth century. As John Boswell has observed, Aelred used the authority of Jesus' relationship with John to justify "the sort of love which had dominated his life." This idealization of friendship represented "a dramatic break with the traditions of monasticism, which had urged since the time of Basil and Benedict that particular friendships of any sort—especially passionate ones—were a threat to monastic harmony and asceticism"; but this new movement was anything but peripheral (225). Saint Anselm, for example, was prior of Bec, the most influential monastery of the period, and later archbishop of Canterbury. He was, says Boswell, "probably the most imposing intellectual figure of his day" (218).

To get a sense for the range of this association between friendship and spirituality in the Judeo-Christian tradition, one has only to consider the numerous references to friendship in the Bible; the various theological arguments that conceive of God as the ultimate friend;[18] the doctrine of brotherly love; or any of a hundred revealing quotations, such as Francis Bacon's suggestion that friendship involves "a kind of civil shrift or confession" (76);[19] Dryden's claim in *The Hind and the Panther* that "friendship of it self an holy tye, / Is made more sacred by adversity" (3.47–48); Fielding's turn on Voltaire's "pious frauds of religion": "pious frauds of friendship" (101); Napoleon's saying, "A faithful friend is a true image of the Deity" (qtd. in B. Stevenson 727); or Nicolas-Sébastien Chamfort's observation that "a man who hides tyranny, patronage, or even charity behind the name and appearance of friendship suggests that infamous priest who poisoned people with holy wafers" (qtd. in Auden and Kronenberger 201).[20]

By the time Emerson and Thoreau were writing their essays on friendship, the religious issue had moved distinctly into the foreground of their concerns. For Emerson, friendship represents the unity of the divine spark (which he believes all of us have) in two people. "Friendship," he says, "demands a religious treatment. . . . Reverence is a great part of it. Treat your friends as a spectacle" (123). Thoreau's idealism has a similar spiritual base. Friendship, he says, "is a miracle which requires constant proofs. It is an exercise of the purest imagination and the rarest faith" (272). For Thoreau friendship actually transfigures reality: "There are passages of affection in our intercourse with mortal men and women . . . which transcend our earthly life" and open up "a new world" for us, "which world cannot else be reached, and does not exist" (268).

The interval from the American transcendentalists to Scott Fitzgerald is less than a century, but it is during this period that the secularization of western culture moved into high gear—so much so that by around the time of the Great Depression Fitzgerald could write in his notebook, "It is in the thirties that we want friends. In the forties we know they won't *save* us any more than love did" (192; emphasis mine). Fitzgerald's pronouncement assumes that a merely human relationship might have held the promise of salvation—an assumption whose very familiarity reveals just how secularized we have become. But measured by historical standards, the idea is shocking indeed, and just how shocking can be seen if we set it beside, say, Martin Luther's attack on standing surety for a friend, as, for example, Antonio did for Bassanio in *The Merchant of Venice*. This practice, by which one person takes a risk for another (as Damon did for Pythias), Luther claims "is a work too lofty for man; it is . . . an invasion of God's rights. For . . . the Scriptures bid us to put our trust and place our reliance on no man, but only on God" (qtd. in Nelson 152). As Benjamin Nelson points out, Luther had a great "hostility to the older friendship *ethos*" precisely because it put so much stock in human—as opposed to divine—relationships (153). Nor was Luther alone in his suspicions. Though the notion of Christ as the divine surety was common in the Middle Ages, and though monastic ideals of friendship reached their zenith in the twelfth century, "deprecations of human friendship as slights to the love of God" were also common, as were later Calvinist attacks on friendship as "idolatry of the flesh" (154).

By now it has become commonplace for us to regard friendship in what, from an historical point of view, can only be seen as a religious context. Few of us have noticed the fact but the evidence seems clear that friendship has, like so many other secular relationships, appropriated to itself functions that traditionally have been understood as religious or spiritual in nature. We turn to friends for consolation in times of trial; we often act out a kind of confession with them, in which we share our deepest dreams and fears along with, in an earlier parlance, our sins;[21] we seek guidance and forgiveness from them, often in conjunction with our confession; we sacrifice for them and they sacrifice for us; we break bread with them in all the ritually charged ways that I described in my last chapter;[22] and in many respects we turn to them as primary sources of meaning and faith. "If one's friends call past midnight with fear like twigs cracking in their voices," says Albert Goldbarth, "one talks faith if one has it or not" (58). The Beatles were surely expressing a widely held conviction in their 1967 song, with its famous refrain, "I get by with a little help from my friends."

None of these functions is new for friendship. What is new is the primacy that they have now assumed: friends have always been sources of consolation, meaning, and faith, but now they seem to be primary sources.[23] And at least one way of suggesting the special flavor of modern loneliness is to observe that friendship has assumed such a spiritual status at a time when numerous other forces—which I briefly discussed in the introduction and first chapter—have made friendship so elusive and problematic. The gap between our sense of the possibilities of friendship and our sense of its difficulties has made our isolation all the more acute.

Andrew Greeley claims that friendship is always "religious behavior in the primordial sense of that word. In the friendship relation we give *ourselves,* and such an offering of the totality of our being is so primordial and intimate that it touches the very roots of our existence and forces us necessarily to face questions of the ultimate" (17). Greeley, though he does not develop a concept of the gift as it relates to friendship, is a Catholic priest and therefore works out of a commitment to the Christian concept of giving up one's life to gain life. "Give and it shall be given unto you" (Luke 6:38), for, according to St. Francis's prayer, "it is in giving that we receive."[24] Though in this sense the concept of friendship as gift exchange seems perfectly compatible with Christian thought, in many other respects, as I have suggested, there is a deep tension between the two. In *Friendship: A Study in Theological Ethics,* Gilbert C. Meilaender focuses on "the central tension between agape and philia," that is, between Christian love and friendship:

> Philia is clearly a preferential bond in which we are drawn by what is attractive or choiceworthy in the friend; agape is to be nonpreferential, like the love of the father in heaven who makes his sun rise on the evil and the good and sends rain on the just and the unjust (Matthew 5:45). Philia is, in addition, a mutual bond, marked by the inner reciprocities of love; agape is to be shown even to the enemy, who, of course, cannot be expected to return such love. Philia is recognized to be subject to

change; agape is to be characterized by the same fidelity which God shows to his covenant. (3)[25]

Meilaender explores these tensions with great sensitivity, and he shows the various respects in which the two ideals offer correctives to each other. But he argues that there is "no fully satisfactory resolution of the tension." His perspective is Christian:

> We must affirm friendship and value its place in human life, not just grant it grudging acceptance in a system which really has no place for it. At the same time we must never fail to note friendship's own limits, against which agape strains. . . . If we rest content in friendship we will fail to see both its source and destination in God. And in failing to see that, we will fail to see friendship for what it is, and we will remove it from the only environment in which it can, finally, flourish. (105–106)

I have tried to show that by adapting Lewis Hyde's theory of gift exchange to friendship we develop a model of understanding that can account for the spiritual dimensions of friendship without recourse to a supernatural deity. For in Hyde's conception, the emphasis is on the circle itself rather than something behind, beyond, or underlying it. There is no prime mover; the emphasis is on the motion itself, on the process of keeping the gift moving. In one sense the gift is the friendship itself, which becomes the pool in which the sentiments of its own exchange accumulate. The spirit that is kept in motion is generated by the friendship itself, and if it becomes a kind of presiding spirit, incarnate in the friendship, it does so only if its human creators do indeed create and sustain it. My earlier analogies between the formal structures of friendship and of art assume in both cases the primacy of man as creator, and in this respect friendship can be seen as a numinous artifact in an age in which art has long been functioning as a secular religion with artists as priests.

"The new fact," according to Nathan Scott, "is . . . that, no longer conceiving themselves to dwell at a point of intersection between Nature and Supernature, the people of our age . . . experience 'the dimension of ultimacy' in and through the claim that is laid upon them by the lives of those others bordering on their own" (35). Glossing Mircea Eliade, among others, Scott claims that "the real center of gravity in the realm of [man's] religious experience . . . is . . . within that network of interpersonal exchange and commonality which forms the matrix of his concrete existence" (16).

We should not be surprised, according to Scott, that the twentieth century has produced so few literary works that show "great examples of men undertaking those special disciplines" of sacrifice for others. After all, we have been "quite unprepared to adduce compelling metaphysical justification of the sacredness of the person," and we have no "sacramentalist view of the human reality" (49). Though Scott admits that André Malraux's work is not grounded in a "fully developed religious position," he considers Malraux a rare and powerful spokesman for *"fraternité*—which commits us to the celebration of the sacrament of the brother" (98–100). In the "consolatory grace" and healing of fraternity, in the "mutual support and comfort of one another," Malraux finds "our surest stay and succor" (61, 73). Though Scott believes Malraux's position is not *"merely* gratuitous," he raises the question asked by one of Malraux's reviewers: "If God is dead, what makes the sacrament of the brother a sacrament?" (99). What, in other words, is the metaphysical rationale for *"fraternité"?* On what grounds should we sacrifice ourselves?

I raise these issues with some hesitation. In the first place, Malraux's ideal of *fraternité,* which he celebrates in such works as *Man's Fate* and *Man's Hope,* differs in important respects from the kind of friendship that I have been examining in this book. In many ways it is much closer to our general sense of human commitment or human fellowship than to friendship itself, in the sense of a concrete, intimate, and ongoing relationship with a particular person. I also hesitate to pose the religious issues so starkly for fear of being misunderstood as arguing that friendship is a new religion, or that it is somehow inconsistent with Christianity or any other theocentric religion, or that friendship is the most important spiritual relationship. I raise these issues because, though friendship has always had spiritual features, we now seem to be in a period during which it increasingly absorbs and appropriates to itself certain functions that traditionally had been considered distinctively religious.

Hyde's theory of gift exchange seems to me especially useful for exploring precisely these elements of friendship, for it does satisfy Scott's requirement of providing a "sacramentalist view of the human reality," at the same time that it provides a metaphysical rationale for both *fraternité* and sacrifice. Moreover, implicit in Hyde's theory of gift exchange is an interesting version of the idea of enlightened self-interest. Though Hyde considers neither the principle of self-interest nor its application to friendship, it is crucial to observe that although the theory of gift exchange argues *against* viewing friends on the economic model of commodities or the political model of power complexes, it need not deny man's inherent self-concern. All along I have been arguing that a theory of friendship which ignores human conflict and self-interest will be as useless by virtue of its naïveté as one that overemphasizes them will be by virtue of its cynicism. In gift exchange, where the gift redounds to the giver, we have a perfect model for friendship at its best. For the fact that the gift does come back to the giver does not mean that it does not come to the recipient, or that the giver's motives are selfish. But neither does it mean that gift exchange takes place in a moral atmosphere so rarified as to make it foreign to the daily round of experience.[26] In this regard, as in so many others, it is Shakespeare who seems to have explored more fully than anyone else the profound connections between both the hard realities and the high ideals of gift exchange and friendship.

3   The Merchant of Venice

"How can the giver of gifts experience the delights of the merchant?"—William Blake, *Visions of the Daughters of Albion*

"A cunning thief will break your money-box and carry off your coin, cruel fire will lay low your ancestral home; your debtor will repudiate interest alike and principal, your sterile crop will not return you the seed you have sown; a false mistress will despoil your treasurer, the wave will overwhelm your ships stored with merchandise. Beyond Fortune's power is any gift made to your friends; only wealth bestowed will you possess always."—Martial, *Epigrams*

The literary master of friendship is, as we might expect, Shakespeare. Hamlet and Horatio, Romeo and Mercutio, Celia and Rosalind, Hal and Falstaff, Hermia and Helena, Brutus and Caesar—these and a dozen other pairs of friends leap immediately to mind. But nowhere else does Shakespeare explore friendship so thoroughly, nowhere else does he define its nature, its aspirations, and its limitations so fully, or praise its greatness so richly, as in *The Merchant of Venice.* And it is in the idea of the gift that Shakespeare finds the most wide-ranging set of metaphors and conceptual complexes with which to explore his subject.

The friendship of Antonio and Bassanio seems straightforward enough. The younger man, Bassanio, has often turned to

Antonio for financial support, and Antonio has always been generous, even if his friend has occasionally been prodigal. Now that Bassanio has a chance to court the wealthy heiress Portia, Antonio will stake him again, even if it means borrowing from the Jewish moneylender Shylock. When Shylock suggests that Antonio pledge a pound of flesh instead of paying the usual interest, Antonio agrees. He is confident that his ships will come in, but he takes a risk nonetheless—in the higher interest of his friendship. When his ships are wrecked and his debt is due, Antonio faces his collector with the equanimity of a man commited to the high ideals of friendship and ready to sacrifice himself for his friend.

Or so it is claimed. For there is quite another way of understanding Antonio's actions. A number of critics have questioned the purity of his motives, pointing to passages that suggest Antonio's homosexual interest in Bassanio or his jealous rivalry with Portia for Bassanio's affections. Some have suggested that in his letter to Bassanio and in his speeches at the trial, Antonio seems all too willing to become a martyr. Other critics have suggested that Portia forces Antonio to undergo a humiliating ceremony of separation at the play's end, in which he acknowledges Portia's victory in the contest for Bassanio's affections and then leaves the stage, sadly alone in contrast to the happy pairs of married lovers. Far from being a selfless sacrificial act, such critics argue, Antonio's contract with Shylock is a desperate ploy to win back Bassanio: it is not a gift but an emotional bribe. Moderate versions of this position see Antonio reverting, perhaps unconsciously, to guilt tactics with Bassanio; stronger versions see him as calculating.[1]

The debate about the quality of Antonio's friendship splits along predictable lines. Those who view Antonio as a true friend tend to see him as a good Christian, utterly pure in motive; they regard the evidence advanced on behalf of the contrary view as a distortion. Those who consider Antonio's motives suspect or tainted, on the other hand, deny that he is a genuine friend and usually accuse his defenders of naïveté. As I suggested earlier, the two major ways of misunderstanding friendship in our time stand at opposite ends of a spectrum: the sentimentalists never see corruption and the cynics see it everywhere. For the one, friendship is a lofty affair of purity, far above any human pettiness; for the other, beneath the fancy claims squirms the all too familiar self-seeking ego. The one idealizes, the other exposes. Where the sentimentalist finds self-sacrifice, the cynic finds guilt-mongering.

The tired polarity of sentimentality and cynicism is not, of course, confined to thinking about friendship, but unfortunately it seems especially characteristic of discourse about friendship. The naive idealization of friendship is particularly troublesome in a culture like ours in which the expectations of friendship are relatively uninstitutionalized, forcing the burden of establishing workable rules on each friendship. Impossibly high ideals are bound to create problems. Equally insidious, however, is the assumption that the only alternative to absolute purity is corruption. As I argued earlier, the mere presence of conflict, envy, aggression, or any number of other contaminants does not doom or invalidate a friendship. It need not even diminish a friendship if the friends can find creative ways of transcending it. And that, as we shall see, is precisely the situation we encounter in *The Merchant of Venice*.

Antonio is not a saint. Like the speaker in many of Shakespeare's sonnets, he is, clearly, upset at some level about the fact that his dear friend Bassanio is in love and will soon be married. "A man's friendships are, like his will, invalidated by marriage," says Samuel Butler, "but they are also no less invalidated by the marriage of his friends" (380). One needn't subscribe to Butler's view or to that of the Ibsen character who claims "a plighted lover cannot be a friend" (103) to acknowledge that in most cases the intensity of friendship cools when one of the friends marries, partly because of the economy of eros (about which more later) and partly because of the economy of time. "In many societies," according to the anthropologist Cora Du Bois, "marriage is considered a crucial threat to pre-existing friendships. . . . The bachelor's party and the best-man custom of Western society are symptomatic of this feeling" (24). There is, in addition, the question of allegiance, of priority, of territory, which is best described by Charles Lamb in his humorous "A Bachelor's Complaint of the Behaviour of Married People." If your old friend is about to court, Lamb warns:

> Look about you—your tenure is precarious—before a twelvemonth shall roll over your head, you shall find your old friend gradually grow cool and altered toward you, and at last seek opportunities of breaking with you. . . . Every long friendship, every old authentic intimacy, must be brought into their [wives'] office to be new stamped with their currency, as a sovereign prince calls in the good old money that was coined in some reign before he was born or thought of, to be new marked and minted with the stamp of his authority, before he will let it pass current in the world. You may guess what luck generally befalls such a rusty piece of metal as I am in these new mintings. (252)[2]

Lamb's economic metaphor accords well with Shakespeare's treatment of the subject in *The Merchant of Venice,* in which usury and money itself take on a profound metaphorical complexity, in which "dear," for example, is used frequently and pointedly as a pun, and in which economic language and themes are at the very center of the play.

But to say that Antonio feels a certain amount of distress at his friend's love and impending marriage is not to say either that his friendship is disguised homosexuality or that it is somehow inauthentic. Some of Antonio's unexplained sadness at the beginning of the play may indeed stem from anxiety that Portia's love might be exclusive, but this fear turns out to be groundless. More important, Antonio acts toward Bassanio in a manner that assumes it is groundless, even if his feelings betray a certain residual uncertainty. To be sure, that uncertainty results in Antonio's all-too-frequent and graphic reminders to Bassanio (in a style that some consider reminiscent of the stereotypical Jewish mother) that he has undertaken this action on his friend's behalf. But these reminders indicate only that Antonio is human, that he has his weaknesses, and that he occasionally indulges himself when restraint would have been the better part of friendship. To conclude from his actions that his friendship is thereby exposed as false seems to me only a bit less ludicrous than to claim that he actually consciously manipulates Bassanio. It is, after all, possible for a friend to transcend his less noble impulses, and it seems to me that is exactly what Antonio does. Seeing him as a schemer is just as inaccurate as seeing him as a saint. He is, rather, a good friend who does indeed feel a bit of a threat but who rises above it to perform an act of great generosity.

In order to argue this case further, I want to establish in detail what seems to me the most important context for considering friendship in this play: the pervasive concern with gift giving. Once we extract our consideration of friendship in *The Merchant of Venice* from the dead-end models of sentimentality and cynicism, and once we see the centrality of gift exchange, we can begin to understand Shakespeare's treatment of friendship in its proper perspective.

In his introduction to the Arden edition of *The Merchant of Venice* John Russell Brown says that the play is "about conundrums such as the more you give, the more you get," and that "giving is the most important part—giving prodigally, without thought for the taking" (1). Brown is by no means the only critic to have observed the importance of this theme; Lawrence Danson, for example, discusses it in relation to Seneca's *De Beneficiis* (50–55).[3] But no one, to my knowledge, has fully explored Shakespeare's elaborate treatment of gift exchange in *The Merchant of Venice*. To do so is to confront some of the play's central cruxes from a fresh and illuminating perspective that, without evading the darker and more troubling aspects of the play, allows one to understand *The Merchant of Venice* as a comedy after all.

This play is utterly dominated by the giving of gifts. The first and most important instance is the money that Antonio borrows from Shylock—at great personal risk—to finance Bassanio's voyage. But from the first encounter between Antonio and Bassanio it becomes clear that many gifts have preceded this one, that Antonio's generosity has been virtually supporting his friend's prodigality. "To you Antonio," says Bassanio,

I owe the most in money and in love,
And from your love I have a warranty
To unburthen all my plots and purposes
How to get clear of all the debts I owe.
(1.1.130–134)

Though Bassanio seems to feel in debt, Antonio's response indicates that he offers his money openly, in the spirit of gift. "Be assured," he says, "My purse, my person my extremest means / Lie all unlock'd to your occasions" (1.1.137–39).

Not least among the expenses that Antonio's money covers is the purchase of gifts to woo Portia. Suitors are coming from everywhere to court this "lady richly left" (1.1.161)—itself a reference to the gift of her father's estate; to compete, Bassanio needs money: "O my Antonio, had I but the means / To hold a rival place with one of them" (1.1.173–74). That a good deal of Antonio's money is spent on gifts is evident from the Messenger's remarks in act 2, scene 9, when she reports to Portia that Bassanio is coming with "gifts of rich value" (90).

Just after he learns that he has chosen the correct casket, Bassanio tells Portia: "fair lady, by your leave, / I come by note to give, and to receive" (3.2.139–40). He has brought his gifts and now it is his turn to receive and Portia's turn to give. Her actual gift to Bassanio is a ring, but what she really gives is herself and her possessions:

Myself, and what is mine, to you and yours
Is now converted. But now I was the lord
Of this fair mansion, master of my servants,
Queen o'er myself: and even now, but now,
This house, these servants, and this same myself
Are yours,—my lord's!—I give them with this ring,
Which when you part from, lose, or give away,
Let it presage the ruin of your love,
And be my vantage to exclaim on you.
(3.2.166–74)

Marriage means that Portia freely gives to Bassanio her purse and person, just as Antonio offered to do. But she also gives her husband the gift of an extraordinary favor: she rescues his best friend. When Portia hears of Antonio's plight, it is clear that money is no object to her:

> Por. What sum owes he the Jew?
> Bass. For me three thousand ducats.
> Por. What no more?
> Pay him six thousand, and deface the bond:
> Double six thousand, and then treble that,
> Before a friend of this description
> Shall lose a hair through Bassanio's fault.
> (3.2.296–301)

The gift, we remember from Hyde, always comes back through indirection, after it has turned a corner. In this instance Antonio's initial gift to Bassanio is answered, as it were, by Portia's intervention, in the guise of the judge, to save Antonio's life.

A parallel gift—but one of a very different flavor—is then given by the Duke of Venice to Shylock. Just before he confiscates Shylock's wealth and property, the Duke presents him with the gift of his life: "That thou shalt see the difference of our spirit / I pardon thee thy life before thou ask it" (4.1.364–65). This is a spiteful gift but a gift nonetheless, as is Shylock's gift to his daughter Jessica and her lover Lorenzo, which he is forced to give by Antonio. Shylock must "record a gift," says Antonio, "(Here in this court) of all he dies possess'd / Unto his son Lorenzo and his daughter" (4.1.384–86).[4] That Shylock takes no joy in receiving or in giving these gifts is certainly understandable; they clearly violate something in the spirit of gift. But in another sense Shylock's antagonism toward gifts here is consistent with his character throughout the play. All along, his possessiveness has been contrasted starkly with Antonio's and Portia's generosity, and his usury has been the very symbol of commodity exchange. When Shylock says "Antonio is a good man," he must explain to Bassanio, who assumed he meant virtuous, that "my meaning in saying he is a good man, is to have you understand me that he is sufficient" (1.3.11, 13–15)—i.e., he will make good on a loan.

The significance of usury in *The Merchant of Venice* has been widely discussed, but for our purposes we need to underline the contrast that Shakespeare establishes between usury on the one hand, and gift giving and friendship on the other. In Elizabethan England, as Brown has shown, "friendship and usury were clearly opposed," and he quotes Sir Thomas Wilson's *A Discourse Upon Usury* (1572) to precisely that effect: "God ordeyned lending for maintenaunce of amitye, and declaration of loue, betwixt man and man: whereas now lending is vsed for pryuate benefit and oppression, & so no charitie is vsed at all" (qtd. in *Merchant* liii–liv). When Antonio is bargaining with Shylock, he tells him:

> If thou wilt lend this money, lend it not
> As to thy friends, for when did friendship take
> A breed for barren metal of his friend?
> (1.3.127–29)

Usury, Antonio suggests, is utterly alien to friendship.

There are two central distinctions between the usurer and the gift giver. First, the usurer enters the exchange in order to add to his own wealth, whereas the giver's intention is to increase the recipient's wealth. Second, in contrast to the gift giver's risk, the usurer's risk is calculated because, at least in Venice, he can prosecute if his debtor fails to pay. In her famous speech, quoted above, in which she pledges herself to Bassanio in marriage, Portia reveals that her desire is not to increase her own various riches:

> You see me Lord Bassanio where I stand,
> Such as I am; though for myself alone
> I would not be ambitious in my wish
> To wish myself much better, yet for you,
> I would be trebled twenty times myself,
> A thousand times more fair, ten thousand times more rich,
> That only to stand high in your account,
> I might in virtues, beauties, livings, friends
> Exceed account: but the full sum of me
> Is sum of something.
> (3.2.149–58)

Portia's riches do increase in every way but they do so precisely because she gives them away. This paradox is closely aligned to a paradox C. L. Barber has observed in this speech: it is "by an elaborate metaphor of accounting, that what is happening sets the accounting principle aside" (177). Shylock could no more understand the paradoxical logic of gift than he could recognize that "the full sum of me" that Portia gives to Bassanio is far greater than the sum of its parts.

Bassanio himself, on the other hand, is beginning to grasp that point, as his response to Portia indicates:

> Madam, you have bereft me of all words,
> Only my blood speaks to you in my veins,
> And there is such confusion in my powers,
> As after some oration fairly spoke
> By a beloved prince, there doth appear
> Among the buzzing pleased multitude,
> Where every something being blent together,
> Turns to a wild of nothing, save of joy
> Express'd, and not express'd: but when this ring
> Parts from this finger, then parts life from hence,—
> O then be bold to say Bassanio's dead!
> (3.2.175–85)

Bassanio senses here the surplus of energy and value that comes along with the gift and constitutes its truest wealth, but he is only beginning to learn that wealth must be risked in the service of love. His first lesson in that education was provided by Antonio's risk taking to secure the money. The second lesson is inscribed on the lead casket, and provides the central link between the subplot of the caskets and the main plot: "Who chooseth me, must give and hazard all he hath" (2.7.9). Antonio did that for Bassanio, and so did Portia. In the trial scene, it appears that Bassanio will do the same for Antonio:

> Bass. Antonio, I am married to a wife
> Which is as dear to me as life itself,
> But life itself, my wife, and all the world,
> Are not with me esteem'd above thy life.
> I would lose all, ay sacrifice them all
> Here to this devil, to deliver you.

Por. Your wife would give you little thanks for that
      If she were by to hear you make the offer.
      (4.1.278–85)

Portia is, of course, "by to hear"; she speaks those lines disguised as the judge. But the irony goes considerably beyond the obvious dramatic one, for in one crucial sense Portia is delighted to hear her husband say that he is willing to risk all for love. It is, to be sure, the love of his friend, not his wife, for which he proposes to sacrifice himself, and he has, after all, just said that he does not value his wife above his friend. Portia is not naive about prospective rivalries and conflicting loyalties of wives and friends. Her intervention on Antonio's behalf is not motivated by self-interest, but she is certainly aware of it, and she knows that her intervention will probably serve it. "For never shall you lie by Portia's side," she says earlier, "with an unquiet soul" (3.2.304–5). But she never feels threatened by Bassanio's friendship with Antonio; on the contrary, she welcomes it, as she explains to Lorenzo:

           For in companions
That do converse and waste the time together,
Whose souls do bear an egall yoke of love,
There must be needs a like proportion
Of lineaments, of manners, and of spirit;
Which makes me think that this Antonio
Being the bosom lover of my lord,
Must needs be like my lord. If it be so,
How little is the cost I have bestowed
In purchasing the semblance of my soul,
From out the state of hellish cruelty!—
This comes too near the praising of myself,
Therefore no more of it.
(3.4.11–23)

Portia realizes that Bassanio's first allegiance must be to marriage, not friendship, but she also has the sense not to pose the issue as a conflict, for she knows that the economy of eros is not strict. No one can accuse Nietzsche of being naive about rivalry, and yet he claims that "the best friend will probably get the best wife, because a good marriage is based on a talent for friendship" (*Human* 295). Portia recognizes that if Bassanio's friendship with Antonio is healthy, her marriage has a better chance of being strong. But self-interest, we recall, is not inconsistent with giving. Portia's sensitivity to the delicacy of that relationship is clear in her embarrassed discovery that "This comes too near the praising of myself." Her recognition that she stands to gain if Bassanio's friendship with Antonio is maintained is partly why Portia includes Antonio in the marriage ceremony at the end, and it is surely one reason why, though she must never admit it, Portia is not really distressed that Bassanio gave away the ring.

Those who argue that Portia is upset by the fact that Bassanio gave the ring away assume that Portia sees herself in competition with Antonio for Bassanio's affections. Ann Barton, for example, claims that "Antonio's hidden jealousy" of Portia comes out in act 4, scene 1, when, resigning himself to what he thinks is his imminent death, Antonio says to Bassanio:

> Commend me to your honourable wife,
> Tell her the process of Antonio's end,
> Say how I lov'd you, speak me fair in death:
> And when the tale is told, bid her be judge
> Whether Bassanio had not once a love.
> (269–73)

"There is almost a sense," says Barton, "that Antonio welcomes death as an incontrovertible proof that he has done something for Bassanio that Portia can never hope to rival, has elevated his love above hers" (252–53). When Bassanio, in his response, says that he values Antonio's life above even his own and his wife's, Portia, according to Barton, "realizes that the situation must be clarified and [thus] resorts to the ring trick: a test which forces Bassanio to weigh his obligations to his wife against those to his friend and to recognize the latent antagonism between them" (253).

If we grant that there is a certain amount of latent antagonism between Antonio and Portia, the question is whether

Portia wants to draw Bassanio's attention to it so that he may reorder his priorities, or whether she wants to find a way for all three of them to transcend the conflict. Though Portia does, by means of the ring trick, establish the priority of marriage over friendship, she does so without exacerbating—indeed by defusing—the antagonism with Antonio. Her intent is to resolve the problem without forcing Bassanio to make a choice. All of Portia's earlier actions and speeches suggest that without being blind to territorial rivalries, she is not caught up in them; and everything about her generous character suggests that she would give both Antonio and Bassanio the benefit of any doubt. Moreover, in every other domain of the plot she has performed the role of grand unifier, descending into the city to protect its law and religion without herself being bound by them. A number of critics have observed that Portia respects forms and conventions but uses them for higher purposes (e.g., Bloom and Tovey), and in this regard I would suggest that she treats symbols, such as the ring, in precisely the same way that she treats law and religion. She must maintain their outward appearance of ultimate authority but she recognizes—as Shylock, for example, does not—that they are conventions meant to serve more important ends.

That Bassanio would give his ring away to the judge who saved Antonio's life is for Portia not an indication of his infidelity to her or of his preference for Antonio over her, but rather of his ability to distinguish convention from the value it serves, and, more important, of his willingness to hazard all for love. Portia arranged the ring trick for two reasons, both of which have equal claim: to provide the opportunity for Bassanio to risk all for his friend and to provide the means for reestablishing her own relationship with him on its proper ground. If justice would censure Bassanio, mercy would forgive. Bassanio really is hazarding all for his friend by giving away the ring, since Portia had earlier told him that giving it away would "presage the ruin of your love" (3.2.173). Bassanio understands that, as he tells the judge, he has made a "vow / That I should neither sell, nor give, nor lose it"—to which Portia, disguised as the judge, replies, "That scuse serves many men to save their gifts" (4.1.438–40). In act 5, speaking in her own person, she refers explicitly to the ring as "your wife's first gift" (5.1.167).

In terms of gift exchange, Portia's ring trick is masterful, for it allows Bassanio to give a gift simultaneously to his friend and to his wife. Both gifts constitute a kind of repayment: Bassanio risks all for Antonio just as Antonio had earlier done for him, and Bassanio gives a ring to Portia (who is, of course, the person beneath the disguise) just as she had earlier given a ring to him. But as always in gift giving, the purpose of the gift is not to settle accounts; rather, the gift is given indirectly—quite graphically in the case of Portia, and more subtly with Antonio.

We remember from Hyde that the gift must be kept moving; it is in this sense, I think, that Bassanio's giving away the ring can be most clearly seen as a positive act for Portia, who herself embodies so much of the spirit of gift giving in the play. Hyde tells us that "the accumulation of capital has its own benefits—security and material comfort being the most obvious and appealing—but the point here is that whatever those benefits, if they flow from the conversion of gifts to capital then the fruits of the gift are lost. At that point property becomes correctly associated with the suppression of liveliness, fertility, and emotion" ("Food" 60). Not to give the ring away would have been tantamount, in these terms, to converting a gift to capital, and it is clear that the security, material comfort, and suppression of liveliness connected with capital are in *The Merchant of Venice* associated with Shylock and contrasted negatively to Antonio's and Portia's imaginative economy of gift.

Though Shylock seems to represent the very antithesis of gift giving, in one memorable instance he reveals that he does understand something of the significance of gifts. When Tubal tells him that Jessica has given away his ring in exchange for a monkey, Shylock responds in a way that is all the more moving to the extent that it seems uncharacteristic:

> Out upon her!—thou torturest me Tubal,—it was
> my turquoise, I had it of Leah when I was a bachelor:

I would not have given it for a wilderness of monkeys.
(3.1.110–13)

Like Dante showing his deep sympathy with Paolo and Francesca despite their violation of the moral order, Shakespeare shatters the symmetry of the gift's schema and allows Shylock's sheer humanity to overwhelm us for a moment. Shylock, who remains blind to the true values of the gift, who is forced to accept a gift (the Duke's pardon) and to give one (to Jessica and Lorenzo), for a shining instant reminds us that even he once accepted a gift in the right spirit, and that at some level its value for him remains, even if he seems incapable of *giving* gifts. (Notice, by the way, that, unlike Bassanio when he gives away Portia's ring, Jessica does not really give away Shylock's ring; she barters it, and—again unlike Bassanio—in flagrant disregard for its symbolic status and value for her father.)

Shakespeare understands that gift exchange both depends on and strengthens the bonds of community, which means that its power can readily become exclusive—a fear that, in another context, complicates Antonio's relationship with Bassanio and Portia. Shylock, as a Jew, is not simply an outsider in Venice; he lies outside all of the structures of community in the play—those based on religion, on friendship, on gift exchange, and even on the final communal dance of comedy at Belmont. But the issue of insiders and outsiders has already been raised by the fact that all of Portia's suitors who precede Bassanio are foreigners: the Neapolitan prince, Count Palatine, the French lord Monsieur Le Bon, the young English baron Falconbridge, the Scottish lord, the German, the Prince of Morocco, and the Prince of Arragon. "There is not one among them but I dote on his very absence" (1.2.105–6), says Portia with regal contempt.

Though Shylock clearly is an outsider in all the senses I have described, in Venice he is, in a strict political sense, considered part of the community, for Venice was "known the world over," according to Allan Bloom, "as the most tolerant city of its time" (14). Antonio recognizes that the law protects outsiders, and that Venice's reputation for justice and commerce is very much at stake in his quarrel with Shylock:

> The duke cannot deny the course of law:
> For the commodity that strangers have
> With us in Venice, if it be denied,
> Will much impeach the justice of the state,
> Since that the trade and profit of the city
> Consisteth of all nations.
> (3.3.26–31)

When Portia, in the trial scene, invokes a law based on the distinction between aliens and citizens, she "turns directly," as Marc Shell observes, "to 'the first and most obvious division of the people,' as William Blackstone says, the division 'into aliens and natural-born subjects.' The turn contradicts a universalist humanistic ethic like that proposed by Christianity" (71).

Shell has in mind here the notion that Christian love (agape) involves universal brotherhood.[5] This is not the place to address the whole vexed question of religion in this play, nor is it the place to attempt a full explanation of the theme of usury. But it is worth noting at least this much: that the Deuteronomic commandment on usury (23:19–20) forbade the Hebrews from practicing usury with their fellow Jews but allowed it with outsiders; and that, as Benjamin Nelson has observed, "medieval Christianity, aspiring to universalism, rejected the Deuteronomic discrimination against the alien as anachronistic and obnoxious, and proposed to transcend the morality of clan by joining the 'other' to the 'brother'" (xxii–xxiii). Antonio, we remember, tells Shylock he hates usury but will go along with it for his friend's sake:

> Shylock, albeit I neither lend nor borrow
> By taking nor by giving of excess,
> Yet to supply the ripe wants of my friend,
> I'll break a custom.
> (1.3.56–59)

In clear violation of the universalist ethic Antonio draws the line very distinctly:

If thou wilt lend this money, lend it not
As to thy friends, for when did friendship take
A breed for barren metal of his friend?
But lend it rather to thine enemy.
(1.3.127–30)

But Shylock says he wants to forgive and forget. "I would be friends with you, and have your love" (1.3.134), he tells Antonio, and he even offers to lend him the money without taking any "doit / of usance" (1.3.136–37). Since a pound of flesh is worthless, Shylock claims, he is making this offer simply in order to be friends: "to buy his favour, I extend this friendship" (1.3.164).

Whether we ought to take Shylock at his word, or whether we ought to see him as plotting to "catch [Antonio] once upon the hip" (1.3.41), the notion of buying favor with friendship must strike us as curious indeed in light of the larger patterns of economic metaphor we have been observing in the play. The whole theme of usury in *The Merchant of Venice* complicates and dramatizes both those patterns and the larger concern with communities, with insiders and outsiders, friends and enemies, citizens and aliens. Shylock's forced conversion to Christianity raises extraordinarily complex and troubling questions in this regard. In one sense, clearly, it is an attempt to make the other a brother. But are we meant to regard this as a perversion of the ideal of gift exchange—a lapse that is related to the Christian practice of slavery in the play and to Antonio's spitting at Shylock, and which we are meant to deplore? Or is Shakespeare suggesting that this is the inevitable underside or cost, in terms of freedom, of adopting a model of gift exchange—a noble but imperfect model, which necessarily has insiders and outsiders? For as Hyde admits, gift exchange "has its negative aspects. Given their bonding power, 'poisonous' gifts . . . must be refused. . . . It is also true that the bonds set up by gift exchange limit our freedom of motion. If a young person wants to leave his or her parents, it's best to stop accepting gifts because they will only maintain the parent-child connection. As gifts are associated with being connected to a community, so commodities are associated with both freedom and rootlessness" ("Food" 34).

In these terms the vexed question that has occupied so many readers and critics can be recast as follows: Does Shakespeare intend the forced conversion to be seen as a true gift or as a poisonous one? Are the cruelties visited on Shylock the inevitable outcome of gift exchange, its dark underside? Or are they merely the result of a flawed application of an otherwise sound ideal? Is there always a hidden cost in gift exchange or only when the ideal has been perverted? These issues are, of course, tied up with the play's concern with the various kinds of exclusiveness and inclusiveness in friendship, marriage, and civil society; with the exploration of bonding and binding, freedom and choice, ownership and membership. We encounter here perplexities that no critic, to my mind, has successfully untangled, and I can go no further than to articulate these questions and issues and to record my confident sense that pursuing them will take us closer to the heart of the play.

Though Shylock's forced conversion may in one way be related to the spiritual economy of gift exchange, Shylock remains indifferent to the other, more attractive features of that economy. A commodity, we remember, earns profit whereas a gift gives increase. "The distinction," says Hyde, "lies in what we might call the vector of the increase: in gift exchange it, the increase, stays in motion and follows the object, while in commodity exchange it stays behind as profit" (*Gift* 37). Shylock, whose ethos is entirely that of commodity exchange, cannot understand that gift exchange has its own principle of increase, which comes, paradoxically, as a result of consumption or spending. "Whatever we are given should be given away again," says Hyde (*Gift* 35). "The gift and its bearers share a spirit which is kept alive by its motion among them and from that the life emerges, willy-nilly" (*Gift* 58).

Shakespeare plays an extraordinary number of variations on this theme of increase, particularly near the end of the play in the bawdy jokes about sexuality and procreation. For our purposes, however, the most interesting variation is his appropriation of usury as a metaphor for love. "It is well known," as W. H. Auden observes, "that love and understanding breed love and understanding.... So, with the rise of a mercantile economy in which money breeds money, it becomes an amusing paradox" for Shakespeare to use such an ignoble activity as a metaphor for "the most noble of human activities" ("Brothers" 230).[6] Conceptually, I would argue, the same point applies to gift exchange, for the giving of gifts turns out to be a kind of spiritual usury in *The Merchant of Venice*. In his *A Discourse Upon Usury,* Sir Thomas Wilson asks, in the name of God, "why didst thou not bestowe my grace and my gifts to the profite of others, by communicating the same among them? Thus spiritual usurie is called the multiplicacion of the giftes and graces of god" (190). Spiritual usury in this sense is of course related to the parable of the talents, and in *The Merchant of Venice* it is mainly tied up with Shylock's forced conversion and Jessica's willing conversion to Christianity. But gift exchange can be seen as a kind of usury in the sense that it increases one's investment and that one can only have one's cake if one eats it.[7] The barren metal of the ring, for example, is made to breed, but only when it is given away—and given away precisely in the service of friendship. Like money, the other "barren metal" in the play, the ring is valuable only when it is, as it were, spent. Like law and religion, coins and rings (or, more generally, symbols, forms, and conventions) are the embodiment of values that do not inhere in them but which depend on them for their circulation.

In a similar fashion, the spirit of gift must circulate through specific gifts. In *The Merchant of Venice* that spirit is closely linked with the spirit of mercy, as Portia describes it during the trial:

> The quality of mercy is not strain'd,
> It droppeth as the gentle rain from heaven
> Upon the place beneath: it is twice blest,
> It blesseth him that gives, and him that takes.
> (4.1.180–83)

We have already seen how the gifts in this play come unstrained and unbidden, and how they bless both the giver and the receiver. It might be useful now, by way of summary, to list the major gifts up to this point in the play:

1. The many gifts that Antonio gives to Bassanio prior to the action of the play.
2. The money Antonio borrows from Shylock for Bassanio.
3. The gifts Bassanio brings to Portia.
4. The estate Portia's father wills to her.
5. The money Jessica gives Lorenzo, a dowry stolen from Shylock.
6. The ring Shylock's wife gives to him.
7. The ring Portia gives to Bassanio.
8. The money and property that Shylock is forced to give Jessica and Lorenzo.
9. The ring Bassanio gives to the judge.
10. The ring Nerissa gives to Gratiano.
11. The ring Gratiano gives to the clerk.

I list here only the major gifts, leaving aside others like the ducat Jessica gives Launcelot when he leaves Shylock's service, or the "dish of doves" (2.2.128) Gobbo brings for Shylock but ends up giving to Bassanio. I am also putting aside, for the moment, such immaterial gifts as Portia's of herself and her possessions to Bassanio, or the Duke's gift to Shylock of his life (through the pardon). The principles of indirection, increase, and continual movement should already be evident; but the gifts do not stop here.

In the first place, Portia does not hold onto the ring; she gives it to Antonio to give to Bassanio. As we near the end of the play, the emphasis on giving increases, as gift follows gift and the very words multiply, as if at the levels of plot and language Shakespeare is driving home his theme of the gift's increase. In the space of some thirty lines, for example, in the play's final scene, the word *gave* appears seven times, *give* once, and *gift* once (5.1.167–200). As Alice N. Benston points out, "If . . . Portia is using the ring trick to teach the men to place friendship below married love, why does Portia involve Antonio in the new bond? Why does he, so to speak, become a member of the wedding? . . . Recalling . . . that the ring passes through Antonio's hands, we should see this last action as a rebinding that incorporates rather than rejects him" (383). It does represent an incorporation rather than rejection of Antonio, but it also, contrary to Benston, subordinates friendship to married love[8]—or perhaps, more precisely, it reveals that male-male friendship has no equivalent to the institution of marriage for romantic love. That is one reason, surely, why Antonio, despite his apparent understanding of the value of marriage, is anxious from the outset: friendship is vulnerable partly because it must be sustained without the institutional support and legal sanction of marriage. It is also less secure, compared with married love, to the extent that it is not sexual. Friendship may be nobler—or at least more selfless—than married love precisely for these reasons, but it remains more vulnerable as well. Antonio can give spiritually and economically, as can Portia, but unlike her, he cannot give sexually.

By giving the ring to Bassanio via Antonio, Portia both follows the logic of indirection that we have already observed in so many of the other transactions of gift exchange, and implicates Antonio in her union with Bassanio, bringing him, as it were, into the force field of their magic circle. She may subordinate Antonio but she does so by bringing him in, not closing him out. In so doing she defuses any potentially explosive conflicts over Bassanio and at the same time reveals that her own generosity comes out of strength and openness—qualities that Antonio demonstrates as well when he pledges his soul for his friend's faithfulness to his wife:

> I once did lend my body for his wealth,
> Which but for him that had your husband's ring
> Had quite miscarried. I dare be bound again,
> My soul upon the forfeit, that your lord
> Will never more break faith advisedly.
> (5.1.249–53)

Antonio will "give away" his friend in marriage, and Bassanio and Portia will "give" themselves to each other in marriage. By offering his soul this time for his dear friend Bassanio, Antonio completes the process of giving and hazarding "all he hath" which he began when he gave the first of the long sequence of gifts in this play: the money he borrowed at such great risk from Shylock.

But even Antonio's pledge of his soul is not the final gift in the play. Nerissa gives both the ring to Gratiano[9] and Shylock's "special deed of gift" (5.1.292) to Jessica and Lorenzo, who refers to it as "manna" (5.1.294), thus associating the gift with mercy, which also falls from heaven. By far the subtlest gift in *The Merchant of Venice* is the one that Portia gives Antonio at the end:

> Antonio you are welcome,
> And I have better news in store for you
> Than you expect: unseal this letter soon,
> There you shall find three of your argosies
> Are richly come to harbour suddenly.
> You shall not know by what strange accident
> I chanced on this letter.
> Ant.   I am dumb!
> (5.1.273–79)

We too are struck dumb by this sudden turn of events. After all, it was in Portia's company that Bassanio asked Salerio, in act 3, scene 2:

> And not one vessel scape the dreadful touch
> Of merchant–marring rocks?
> Sal.   Not one my lord.
> (269–70)

It is a "strange accident" indeed—too strange, finally, to be credible, even if we grant that happy reversals are commonplace in comedy. How, after all, did Portia know the contents of the letter if it was sealed? One can understand why Portia might not want to explain the accident then and there, but one has to wonder why she makes a point of telling Antonio that he "shall not know" the explanation. We need not literalize the point, but at least in terms of its figurative effect, it seems clear that Portia is giving a gift to Antonio. For it is she, in fact, who seems to be providing for Antonio here. Just as she earlier disguised herself on his behalf, she now disguises her gift for him as a piece of good fortune. "Sweet lady,"

Antonio tells her, "you have given me life and living" (5.1.286). Why does Antonio say that it was Portia who gave this to him? Presumably, she gave him the good news, not the goods themselves. Is there some level at which he knows that this is Portia's gift? Is he respecting the propriety of not referring directly to that fact, just as she has maintained the fiction that she is merely reporting his good fortune?

The cumulative power of the gift has become so strong by the end of *The Merchant of Venice* that one has an almost magical sense of riches and bounty. Belmont is transformed into the kind of fairyland in which, even at a material level, the more one gives, the more one gets. Vast sums, it seems, are flowing all ways in this cornucopia, whose fertility, fecundity, and sheer joy stand as the final emblems for the spirit of gift, and the world of comic fruition with which it is identified.

There is, nonetheless, as so many critics have observed, something sad about Antonio standing alone on stage at the play's end while all the others pair off in couples. In this respect he becomes a strange counterpart to that other merchant of Venice, Shylock. But it is precisely to ease his pain that Portia gives Antonio the gift, and there is no denying that it serves as a kind of compensation for Antonio. "I have engag'd myself to a dear friend," Bassanio tells Portia earlier in the play, with dramatically ironic puns on both *engag'd* and *dear* (3.2.260). The puns on *dear* continue:

Por. Is it your dear friend that is thus in trouble?
Bass. The dearest friend to me, the kindest man.
(3.2.290–91)

Antonio is both cherished and expensive, but so is Bassanio, as Portia acknowledges a few lines later in still another set of these puns: "since you are dear bought, I will love you dear" (3.2.312). Portia realizes that loving Bassanio dear means preserving his friendship with Antonio, which she did earlier by saving Antonio's life and does now by ministering to his spirit. "How little is the cost I have bestowed," she tells Lorenzo, "In purchasing the semblance of my soul" (3.4.19–20).

But Portia seems keenly aware that it would be ill-advised

to present Antonio's fortune to him as a gift. In one sense, of course, this is a perfect example of a gift coming back to one after turning a corner; it is not simply Antonio's due but a token of his value as a friend. But only by making it *seem* his proper due can she avoid making him feel like someone who has to be repaid for something he lost. There is, of course, another sense in which that is exactly what Portia is doing, but she wants to avoid making him feel like an object of pity. Nor does she want him to feel that he is in her debt. In both of these respects there is a direct analogy with the women of *Cranford,* who also—though more literally—disguise their gift to Miss Matty as good fortune. "Benefits which cannot be repaid, and obligations which cannot be discharged, are not commonly found to increase affection," says Dr. Johnson. "Thus imperfect are all earthly blessings; the great effect of friendship is beneficence, yet by the first act of uncommon kindness it is endangered, like plants that bear their fruit and die" (314). Some critics have suggested that Antonio manipulates Bassanio's emotions by putting him in his debt, or at the very least that Bassanio feels guilty as a result of Antonio's extraordinary act of generosity. True gifts are not easy to accept, but that is not to say they are impossible to accept. Whatever uneasiness Bassanio may have felt about Antonio's gift has presumably not been lost on Portia, and it is partly for that reason that she takes such pains to avoid putting Antonio in the position with regard to her that Bassanio had been in with regard to Antonio.

Johnson's argument smacks too much of balancing accounts to seem compatible with the model of gift exchange that, I have been arguing, governs these sensitive transactions. Portia's object, however, is not to even accounts but rather to preserve her husband's friendship with Antonio, which requires a very delicate handling of her own relationship with Antonio. And Johnson does have a point. Though the friendship of Antonio and Bassanio was not ruined by these conflicts, certainly the strains were real. By acting tactfully in these circumstances Portia has managed to give Antonio a double gift: the actual fortune and the sense that it is rightfully his.

Johnson's dictum and my point about Antonio receiving his due would suggest that Antonio's final dispensation is aligned with justice, whereas gift exchange, as I suggested earlier, is associated with mercy. But notice, as Benston observes, that "it is justice—law—not mercy that prevails under Portia's direction at the trial. . . . because Portia does not argue that it become a state policy displacing the law, mercy is all the more protected as the higher virtue" (374). Similarly, it seems to me, the power of the gift is all the more evident at the end of the play to the extent that it has accomplished a kind of justice. By securing Antonio's "life and living," for example, Portia dispenses both justice and mercy: justice, by returning to Antonio what he was bound for—his "life"; and mercy, by giving him his money—his "living." Portia is a master of convention and form, and like her creator, she understands the life-giving powers of disguises and fictions.

Because both mercy and friendship find their characterizing metaphor in the idea of the gift, it is no exaggeration to say that Shakespeare's understanding of friendship in *The Merchant of Venice* is closely related to his understanding of the distinction between both revenge and mercy, and justice and mercy. If mercy is identified with gift exchange, revenge is equally identified with commodity exchange, because, in exacting an eye for an eye, its central concern is to balance the accounts, without any enhancement of value. "When people are friends," says Aristotle, "they have no need of justice, but when they are just, they need friendship in addition" (215). The political, for Aristotle, was a sphere in which the bonds of philia not only operated, but actually provided the basis for what we would now call self-fulfillment. The Venice of this play, on the contrary, was founded on modern liberal principles: tolerance for a variety of groups, and the belief that politics is not an arena for self-fulfillment but a kind of neutral zone in which individuals have certain rights that make possible a private life in which one may seek personal fulfillment. "The fellow-citizen bond," as Meilaender has observed in general about the modern political world, "precisely because it must concern itself with justice, is not a *per-*

sonal bond" (74). This is why Portia relies on justice at the trial and in the process preserves mercy as the higher virtue. For just as, in Aristotle's formulation, justice is insufficient without friendship, so too, Shakespeare suggests, is it insufficient without mercy. The friendly world of Belmont may not require justice; but in Venice, where all kinds of different groups live—not always in friendship—justice is necessary, though its efficacy and certainly its value require that it be seasoned with mercy.[10]

Gift exchange in *The Merchant of Venice* relates not only to the theme of friendship but more broadly to the great questions of value and spirituality that the play dramatizes. The relationships between justice and mercy, between punishment and reward, between sacrifice and self-interest—all of these, along with the vexed political and moral issues of pluralism and tolerance, are tied up with and illuminated by the economy of gift exchange. For our purposes, however, it is the relationship between gift exchange and friendship that is crucial, and that has therefore occupied our attention here. The position I have been advancing is that gift exchange provides the means for the kind of sacrifice, risk, and creative transcendence of conflict that, I have been suggesting, defines the friendships of *The Merchant of Venice*. I want to return briefly to some of the objections to the claim that we are presented with solid and admirable friendship in this play. In so doing I hope to show that the model of gift exchange also provides a way of obviating the polar dangers of sentimentality and cynicism.

There is, first of all, the issue of homosexuality. Graham Midgley says flatly that Antonio "is an unconscious homosexual," and that the most striking "fact" about him "is his all-absorbing love of Bassanio, his complete lack of interest in women—in a play where this interest guides the actions of all the other males—and his being left without a mate in a play which is rounded off by a full-scale mating denouement" (199). Only a few critics have tried to develop a case for the homosexual inclinations of Antonio but many have suggested that such a case would not be inappropriate. Auden, for example, points out that in Dante there is an "association of usury with sodomy," so that it is no accident, he says, that Antonio's emotional life "is concentrated upon a member of his own sex" ("Brothers" 231). Though the association through usury seems dubious, certainly the point about Antonio's emotional life is unarguable, and some critics have seen that as the most convincing explanation of Antonio's unexplained sadness at the beginning of the play.[11] Shakespeare may well be suggesting that at some level there is sexual attraction between Antonio and Bassanio but he can scarcely be said to have gone beyond that. Shakespeare develops the theme along two other important lines: risk and disguise. Had Bassanio not chosen the right casket, he too, like the other unsuccessful suitors, would presumably have been condemned to celibacy; in these terms, then, he stakes his sexual future on heterosexuality, and he wins.

I said earlier that Portia has a deep understanding of the relationship between the conventional and the natural, and that she acts on behalf of law, religion, and the symbolic at the same time that she recognizes their limitations. This understanding on her part also extends to sexuality. That males acted the roles of females in Elizabethan England, and that Elizabethan, especially Shakespearean, drama is full of plays in which women disguise themselves as men, does not mean that Shakespeare cannot exploit such conventions for his own thematic purposes, even when the theme is the status of convention itself. On the contrary, it is precisely because there are such dramatic conventions that Shakespeare can play such fascinating and subtle variations with them. Portia's ultimate object in assuming a male disguise is to save the life of her husband's friend and thus his friendship (and, in a way, her marriage). If there is a sense in which Portia knows she has the upper hand over Antonio it is that her relationship with Bassanio, unlike Antonio's, is sexual. That distinction between the sexes is based on nature, Shakespeare seems to be saying, but many of the other distinctions are merely conventional. Those Portia is quite ready to accommodate to her own purposes. It is because she recognizes, for example, that convention vests judicial authority only in men that she disguises herself as a man. In the final scene of the play, Shakespeare underlines the conventionality of sexual roles through the playful device of dramatic irony. Bassanio and Gratiano still do not know that the judge and clerk to whom they gave their rings were in fact Portia and Nerissa.

> Ner. Gave it a judge's clerk! no—God's my judge—
> The clerk will ne'er wear hair on's face that had it.
> Gra. He will, and if he live to be a man.
> Ner. Ay, if a woman live to be a man.
> (5.1.157-60)

Portia teases Bassanio in the same fashion. "I'll die for't" she tells him, "but some woman had the ring!" (208) "No," cries Bassanio, "by my honour madam, by my soul / No woman had it, but a civil doctor" (209-10). Shakespeare is treating sexuality very playfully here, but the conflict between all male and male-female love runs like an undercurrent throughout these bawdy games, just as it has throughout the play in Bassanio's juxtaposed relationships with Antonio and Portia. After the threat of cuckoldry looms and then is dissipated, when the women confess their trick, Bassanio says to Portia:

> Sweet doctor, you shall be my bedfellow,—
> When I am absent then lie with my wife.
> (5.1.284-85)

Here the undercurrent rises to the surface, but Shakespeare diffuses it at exactly that instant by turning it into still another elaborate joke based on the bafflements of appearance and reality which all along have been informing the development of the play's language, themes, and plot.

In this way, I think, Shakespeare suggests that whatever sexual attraction may be present between Antonio and Bassanio is not in itself a very useful clue to understanding their relationship. Even if there is sexual attraction or desire, it exists within an elaborate complex of physical, emotional, and intellectual attractions that cannot be explained by any single component. To try to peel off the layers of disguise and convention and find exposed a naked sexuality is to miss the whole point of disguises, conventions, and fictions in this play. That "bottom-line" model of explaining human behavior is as alien to Shakespeare's view in *The Merchant of Venice* as is the strict accounting principle and strict constructionism of Shylock. We can grant a certain degree of homosexual concern in the play without in any way assuming that to do so is to explain what is fundamental to the friendship.

In another sense, Shakespeare subordinates whatever homosexuality may have been present to heterosexuality by ending the play with numerous references to procreation and breeding, themes which take on a new literalness at this point after serving so metaphorically, in terms of usury, earlier in the play. Procreation, which is here tied in to the whole consideration of spiritual increase that is associated with gift exchange, is identified with heterosexual love and celebrated, following comic convention, in the prospect of fertile marriage. In this regard there is probably something symbolic in Antonio's movement from pledging his body for Bassanio early in the play to pledging his soul as the play moves to its end. Like his conflict with Portia, any homosexual impulse on the part of Antonio has been transformed into an impulse toward spiritual unity, and though some may view this transformation as simple repression, Shakespeare seems to valorize it by expressing it as a movement from body to soul.

Antonio's occasional recourse to guilt tactics can also be understood along these general lines. As Allan Bloom has remarked, Antonio is "not entirely averse to martyrdom. It fits with his general melancholy, and he can prove his great love by dying for Bassanio. He can make an ever-living memorial for himself in the guilt of his friend" (27). But it is a long way from that observation to Barbara Tovey's claim that Antonio wants Bassanio to "spend the rest of his life in remorseful remembrance." "Hereafter," she says, "Bassanio's function in life will be to serve as an apostle to the 'crucified' Antonio, who dies for his sake" (225). Tovey is suggesting an interesting turn on the common interpretation of Antonio's sacrifice as a Christ-like redemption of Bassanio or, as Benjamin Nelson has argued in regard to Antonio's suretyship to Shylock, an imitation of the prototype of "Christ's act in serving as 'ransom' to the Devil for all mankind" (144n). Tovey offers a more satanic reading: "If Antonio had been allowed to sacrifice himself, Bassanio would have incurred an enormous indebtedness which could only have been repaid by a lifetime of remorseful gratitude" (233). Tovey is quite right to note that Antonio's sacrifice places a considerable burden on his friend, and that that burden would have been virtually intolerable had Antonio actually died on his behalf. But it is another matter altogether to suggest, as she does, that Antonio's motives are entirely selfish and that he does "everything possible to intensify the . . . sense of indebtedness that Bassanio feels toward him" (222). By suggesting that Antonio's object is to increase Bassanio's sense of indebtedness, Tovey not only denies that Antonio's sacrifice constitutes a gift; she actually argues that in fact it is a bribe, an attempt to buy Bassanio's love. If she is right, then Antonio's friendship for Bassanio has the same status as Shylock's for Antonio when Shylock says, "To buy his favour, I extend this friendship" (1.3.164). More important, if Tovey is right, there is no true gift exchange in the play but only commodity exchange masquerading as gift exchange.

Again we find our familiar pattern of answering what seems to be a sentimental concept of friendship with one that is utterly cynical. For Tovey assumes that if there is the slightest trace of self-interest in a sacrificial act, it must be fraudulent and manipulative. Either Antonio is utterly selfless or he is calculating his own interest. But between these poles is a rather considerable moral territory, and it is precisely there, I would argue, that most sacrificial acts take place. Antonio's sacrifice for Bassanio is not an act of Christian agape; it is an act of philia, and as such it stands in a certain tension with agape. Gilbert C. Meilaender does not consider *The Merchant of Venice,* but we recall that he does focus on the "various angles," as he puts it, from which one can see that tension: philia is preferential, changeable and reciprocal, whereas agape is nonpreferential, unchanging, and not necessarily reciprocal (3). Compared with Christian agape, Antonio's love for Bassanio is unquestionably self-interested, but compared with the mercantile utilitarianism embodied in Shylock, Antonio is remarkably selfless. If the former seems sentimental and the latter cynical, neither adequately describes Antonio, for his gift giving contains a principle of self-interest but emphatically subordinates it to the principle of sacrifice.

No one can legitimately deny that Antonio is anxious about Bassanio's love for Portia or that he does seem a bit too ready, at times, to accept his imminent doom. "I am a tainted wether of the flock," he says in the trial scene:

> Meetest for death,—the weakest kind of fruit
> Drops earliest to the ground, and so let me;
> You cannot better be employ'd Bassanio,
> Than to live still and write mine epitaph.
> (4.1.114–18)

In this speech he certainly does indulge in self-pity and, insensitive to the effect of his words on his friend, he romanticizes his situation. But to resign oneself to a fate that seems inevitable, even to romanticize that fate as Antonio does here and elsewhere, scarcely constitutes calculated manipulation of one's friend. Besides, those who dwell on the passages in which Antonio seems to welcome his fate, conveniently forget that in act 3, scene 3, he twice tries to make his case to Shylock (3, 11), only to be met with Shylock's insistent rebuff, "I'll have my bond" (4, 12). Antonio has learned firsthand just how stubbornly Shylock is set on his destruction, and that knowledge, combined with his recent business losses, has made him weary:

> These griefs and losses have so bated me
> That I shall hardly spare a pound of flesh
> To-morrow, to my bloody creditor.
> (3.3.32–34)

In act 4, then, when we no longer see Antonio resisting, what we are witnessing is not delight in martyrdom or the prospect of having Bassanio in his debt, but rather a kind of stoic acceptance of an apparently wretched fate:

> Make no moe offers, use no further means,
> But with all brief and plain conveniency

Let me have judgment, and the Jew his will!
(4.1.81–83)

Just as Shylock begins to sharpen his knife and prepare the scales to weigh the flesh, the judge asks Antonio if he has anything to say:

> Ant. But little; I am arm'd and well prepar'd,—
> Give me your hand Bassanio, fare you well,
> Grieve not that I am fall'n to this for you.
> (4.1.260–62)

In these lines, says Tovey, Antonio suggests that the blame for his fate lies with Bassanio. After all, she points out, doesn't Antonio go on to say of himself that "he repents not that he pays *your* debt" (4.1.275; emphasis Tovey's)? And did not Antonio earlier, in his letter to Bassanio, say that "debts are clear'd between you and I" (3.2.317), as though there were indeed a debt? For Tovey all of these instances reveal Antonio's selflessness to be mere "pretense" (225). In fact, she argues, by urging his friend to witness his death, Antonio acts with cruel selfishness, never considering how such a sight would affect Bassanio's future happiness. If Antonio cared about Bassanio as a friend, says Tovey, he would have followed Aristotle's advice of avoiding causing pain to one's friends, tried to keep Bassanio away from the scene of death, and attempted "to mitigate Bassanio's sense of guilt" (226).

Tovey touches here on important issues, and her argument, exaggerated and distorted as it finally seems to me to be, cannot be treated lightly. But Antonio's reference in the letter to Bassanio's debt, far from being a self-interested attempt to establish that Bassanio *had* owed him a debt, seems to me intended precisely to "mitigate Bassanio's sense of guilt" by assuring him that he does not have a debt to Antonio. That he puts it in those terms indicates not that he never meant his favor as a gift, but that Bassanio would probably still be finding it difficult to accept it as a gift. In the very first scene of the play, we remember, Bassanio says "to you Antonio / I owe the most in money and in love," and he presents Antonio with a plan that will have the fringe benefit of getting himself "clear of all the debts I owe" (1.1.130–31, 134). During the course of the play, Bassanio does indeed get an education in gift exchange, but at this point it is not complete. Antonio knows that if Bassanio were to witness his death it would cause him pain; but it would also, he feels, provide him an invaluable lesson in the meaning of sacrifice.

But would learning the lesson justify the pain? Here we encounter complexities of motive that are impossible to unravel. For there does exist a certain self-regarding impulse in Antonio's letter to Bassanio inviting him to witness his death. However else one might explain Antonio's occasional romanticizing of his cruel fate and his repeated references to Bassanio's debt, they do indeed seem to reveal a kind of self-concern, particularly because in the letter he explicitly links Bassanio's debt with witnessing Antonio's death: "debts are clear'd between you and I, if I might but see you at my death: notwithstanding, use your pleasure,—if your love do not persuade you to come, let not my letter" (3.2.317–20). That last stricture, by its very denial that he wants Bassanio to come out of obligation, clearly must have the effect of intensifying Bassanio's sense of obligation.

There can be no question that we have here a pattern of weakness on Antonio's part, which partly results from the fact that most of the gifts have been given by Antonio. This imbalance in his relationship with Bassanio seems to have an adverse effect upon Antonio's sense of his own worth, which would help explain not only his occasional tentativeness and ambivalence with regard to Bassanio but also perhaps his mysterious sadness. But even if Antonio does sometimes feel a bit taken for granted, he still cares deeply for Bassanio, and in the course of the play Bassanio comes to take Antonio less and less for granted as he comes to understand what it means to give a gift.

In any case, Antonio's weakness—or occasional tentativeness and ambivalence—does not constitute manipulation, and neither does it expose his friendship as fraudulent. What Tovey fails to see—and what Shakespeare is so brilliant at dramatizing—is that it is possible for someone to betray a measure of self-concern and at the same time, without contradiction, undertake a genuine sacrifice. True friends, Shakespeare suggests, do not display saintly perfection; but they do transcend their limitations. Friendship is rare and valuable not because perfection is rare, but because it is difficult for humans to rise above their weaknesses. Actions based on sacrifice and risk, like the larger model of gift exchange, which, I have been arguing, subsumes them in this play, are not utterly unselfish—except, perhaps, in the rare instances of true saints.

But there is another option besides saintly disinterestedness on the one hand and cynical self-interest on the other. In this play, that option is embodied in Bassanio's and Portia's gift giving, but most importantly in Antonio's, which shares with the others' not only genuine risk taking and sacrifice but also a degree of self-interest. According to our model of gift exchange, something always comes back to the giver, so we should not be surprised to discover an element of self-interest in the process. "It is as if you give a part of your substance to your gift partner," says Hyde, "and then wait in silence until he gives you a part of his" ("Food" 44).[12] The issue is whether Antonio, for example, sacrifices in order to advance his own ends, and the answer, clearly, is that he does not. That his own ends are advanced is consistent with the logic of the gift. That he displays something less than a perfectly selfless nature along the way is a simple consequence of his being human. Mark Twain once remarked that there is no laughter in heaven. Why should there be in a perfect place? We might also observe that there would be no sacrifices or gifts in heaven for, like laughter, they arise from imperfect conditions and are valuable precisely because of that fact. The very concept of a gift or a sacrifice includes the idea of anomaly, for it assumes a normal course of behavior that is happily violated. Antonio's sacrifice is not less heroic, or less a sacrifice, because of his occasional self-regard; on the contrary, it is all the more heroic, for it has been more dearly bought.

Throughout the play, it has been clear that anything of value can be won only through great risk. Even in the very first scene, when Salerio and Solanio are talking with Antonio about his ventures at sea, "the accent of their wonder," as Arthur Kirsch has observed, "like their metaphors of the sea, falls upon risk and hazard and peril, and this note is sustained until the very end of the play, when Antonio's ships come home." Antonio's wealth depends on risk. "His friends," says Kirsch, "worry about it, his enemy harps upon it, and the very plot of the play demonstrates it" (15). We have already seen how both Portia and Bassanio also hazard all for love, but it is worth noting in this connection the contrast with Shylock. As Marc Shell has pointed out, Shylock does have the choice of killing Antonio, albeit at the price of losing his own life and property. He decides not to hazard all; instead, merchantlike, he opts for a bargain (70–71).

The inscription on the lead casket, "Who chooseth me, must give and hazard all he hath" (2.7.9), not only links the subplot and the main plot; it also becomes itself a gift from Portia's father: the gift of a teaching about the importance and relation of giving and risking. It is the same teaching—and in that sense the same gift—that Antonio gives Bassanio, for in the course of the play Bassanio comes to understand not just Antonio's and Portia's love for him but love in general. Bassanio, that is to say, learns both how to accept gifts from and how to give gifts to Antonio and Portia. From an initial feeling of being in debt to Antonio, Bassanio moves to a recognition of the extraordinary difficulty of giving, particularly, as in the case of the ring, when that act involves great risk. But he also comes to see how bountiful are its rewards, and in the process he comes to understand and participate in the larger spirit of gift that moves through the play.[13]

That spirit finds its deepest dramatic embodiment in the relationship between two types of bonds in the play: the kind Antonio establishes with Shylock and the kind Bassanio establishes with Portia. "The first," says Benston, "makes possible the interaction among strangers, even enemies, as Antonio observes, while the second [marriage] requires love. . . . no contract will secure love" (382n). In that sense, the distinction is clear and it follows the lines of the parallel distinction between commodity and gift exchange. But there is another sense in which marriage shares with the commercial bond a straightforward legal obligation to remain faithful to the contract, which in the case of marriage means limiting one's freedom of action. Portia could tolerate—even honor— Bassanio giving away her ring earlier because she had devised a game in which everyone would turn out a winner and the gift could be kept moving. In marriage itself, however, there is one clear sense—the sexual—in which one must not keep the gift moving, in which one pledges precisely to limit the circle to husband and wife. The bawdy humor at the end of the play is meant to dramatize that fact and to give vent to—at the same time that it tames—the fear of cuckoldry. That bawdiness also hints playfully at the fact that Portia and Bassanio are about to go off to bed, suggesting still another, this time sexual, gift exchange. The ring, of course, is both a sexual pun and a symbol of the marriage union which domesticates the sexuality. In this sense, it is precisely through sacrificing a certain kind of freedom—through "forsaking all others"—that the gift is kept moving in marriage.

That act of forbearance involves a commitment to the partner which takes the form of a gift if the couple is united by a bond of love. The principle of sacrifice is crucial here, for it is directly related to the risk taking and the specifically sacrificial nature of friendship throughout the play. Bassanio is coming to understand the message of John 15:13: "Greater love hath no man than this, that a man lay down his life for his friends."[14] But there is always the danger of the bond becoming bondage, of the relationship becoming merely a binding contract—like the form that is not animated by any creative spirit and thus becomes, as we say, "mere form." Shakespeare shows us a similar contrast at the level of the law, which can embody a spirit or, as in the case of Shylock, can be a slave to the letter. A marriage open to friendship no more compromises its authority than does a system of justice that is open to mercy.

As Portia knows so well, and as I demonstrated in my first chapter, forms and conventions—laws and marriages included—

have the potential to be both constricting and liberating. So long as they are life giving, so long as they avoid the sterile legalism and narrow vision of a Shylock, forms serve the highest values, including human intimacy. The formal intricacies of Portia's father's will, the elaborate rituals of the casket, the ring game, the oaths, the complex transactions of gift giving, and the artful use of disguises and fictions—all of these involve the playful and creative use of form for important human purposes. Like their counterparts, commercial bonds, the bonds of love are highly formal constructs, not only in marriage but also in friendship, which is also subject to the ambiguity of bonds, as we have already seen with Antonio and Bassanio. Notice the recurrence of the word *bound* as Bassanio introduces his friend to Portia in the last act:

> Bass. I thank you madam,—give welcome to my friend,—
> This is the man, this is Antonio,
> To whom I am so infinitely bound.
> Por. You should in all sense be much bound to him,
> For (as I hear) he was much bound for you.
> Ant. No more than I am well acquitted of.
> (5.1.133–38)

Like marriages, friendships can decay from lively bonding to sterile binding or bondage if the spirit of gift is not preserved. Nor, as I suggested earlier, can friendship depend on a formal institution analogous to that of marriage. In western societies friendship is much more deeply associated with the voluntary than love is, both in terms of choosing one's friends and in terms of breaking off a relationship (friendship has no analogue to divorce). Antonio may have feared that Portia would be a possessive wife, but he comes to see that without relinquishing her claim to Bassanio, she still can avoid being possessive. To do so requires the same kind of wisdom that enables her to distinguish justice from mercy, and commodity exchange from gift exchange. It requires the same kind of self-sacrifice that mercy and the gift involve. And it requires the ability to use forms creatively. Antonio is a stranger to none of these arts. That is why he and Portia understand each other, and that is why he is such an extraordinary friend to Bassanio.

By focusing his dramatic exploration of friendship on form and gift exchange, Shakespeare taps, in *The Merchant of Venice,* the mysteries of both art and religion. It is no accident that form relates so directly to the artistic, and gift to the spiritual, for form and gift draw on the deepest sources of cultural and personal energy, and they share the profound paradoxes of art and religion. As we have seen throughout this book, what is given away or formed does not decrease wealth or freedom; on the contrary, in art freedom comes only through form; and in matters of the spirit, wealth comes only through giving. In friendship, as in the other arts, form works when it is used creatively, and the creative spirit, as Shakespeare knew so well, is itself the spirit of gift.

Notes

Introduction

1   Sex, on the other hand, has, as Michel Foucault has argued, been spoken and written about in modern western society "ad infinitum" even as it has been exploited "as *the* secret" (35). About sex, he says, "an immense verbosity is what our civilization has required and organized. Surely no other type of society has ever accumulated . . . a similar quantity of discourses concerned with sex. It may well be that we talk about sex more than anything else" (33).

1   Friendship and Form

1   Though Brain's major interest is in the social institutions that express the impulse toward friendship, rather than in the kinds of private individual friendships that comprise my own center of attention, his book has been extremely useful to me as a comparative, cross-cultural analysis of friendship.
2   De Tocqueville goes on to observe that "in aristocracies the observance of forms was superstitious; among us they ought to be kept up with a deliberate and enlightened deference" (344).
3   "Broadly speaking," says Horst Hutter, "societies have attempted to cope with the problems posed to social institutions by friendship in two ways: On the one hand, friendship has been defined as lying within the private sphere of life, as being a personal matter for individuals, something that does not fall within the purview of societal regulation. Our own society most nearly approaches this model. . . . On the other hand, in many

societies, friendship has been and is virtually defined as a public institution and is officially regulated. Rules of friendship behaviour are clearly defined, and friends have official status" (8). Robert Paine asks, "How does our kind of friendship flourish without institutionalization?" The prerequisite, he says, is "the existence in the society of an efficient and dispassionate *bureaucracy* so that an individual can enjoy private and uncompetitive relations without prejudice to his other relations that belong to the competitive public sector" (137).

4 One measure of changing conventions in this regard is the final episode of the television series *MASH*, in which Hawkeye and B.J. do indeed hug when they say good-bye, though still with something of the old backslapping male bravado.

5 One way of seeing the reunion meal, or the friendship meal generally, is as a secular version of the early Christian love feast, known as the Agape.

6 C. S. Lewis seems to me much more precise on this point when he speaks of "the exquisite arbitrariness and irresponsibility" of friendship. "Friendship," he says, "is unnecessary, like philosophy, like art, like the universe itself (for God did not need to create)" (84).

7 Cf. C. S. Lewis: "People who simply 'want friends' can never make any. The very condition of having friends is that we should want something else besides friends" (79).

8 Proverbs 27:17 (King James version). Compare the following: "Each friend represents a world in us, a world possibly not born until they arrive, and it is only by this meeting that a new world is born" (Anaïs Nin 2.193). "One who does not see the whole world in his friends / Does not deserve to have the world hear of him" (Goethe I.447–48, pp. 503–4). "Whoever you are, it is your friends who make your world" (Ralph Burton Perry, *The Thought and Character of William James*, cited in Bartlett 649).

9 Cf. John Selden's remark: "Old friends are best. King James used to call for his old shoes, for they were easiest for his feet" (cited in Burton Stevenson 738); and the ancient Chinese verse:

> The ideal state of friendship:
> At the first meeting to feel like old friends;
> In old age, to remain fresh and enjoyable.
> (cited in Lai 9)

10 Intensity also has something to do with alleviating suffering, in the sense Keats suggests in his famous "vale of Soul-making" letter (2:100–104).

11 Cf. Keats: "the first political duty a Man ought to have a Mind to is the happiness of his friends" (2.213). Creon states just the opposite view in Sophocles' *Antigone:* "And he who counts an-

other greater friend / than his own fatherland, I put him nowhere" (182-83).

12 For C. S. Lewis this shared perspective leads not to comedy but to a threat to authority. "Every real Friendship," he says, "is a sort of secession, even a rebellion. . . . In each knot of Friends there is a sectional 'public opinion' which fortifies its members against the public opinion of the community in general. Each therefore is a pocket of potential resistance. Men who have real Friends are less easy to manage or 'get at'; harder for good Authorities to correct or for bad Authorities to corrupt" (94). Solzhenitsyn's memoirs of his relationship with Tvardovsky, the editor of *Novy Mir,* demonstrate the dramatic complexities of this theme as it interacts with the prospects of betrayal. (See *The Oak and The Calf.*) George Steiner's fine essay on Anthony Blunt also sheds light on this issue.

13 An interesting parallel can be drawn between the insulting game and the prank or practical joke. In both cases the breaking of rules that are usually in force serves to affirm intimacy and generate trust. For a fascinating discussion of the healthy and highly ritualized function of insults among Black Americans, see Abrahams.

14 Cf. Guy de Maupassant's short story "Friend Joseph," in which two childhood friends—one now very wealthy and the other a bourgeois radical—meet many years later. The rich one invites his old friend to his country house and tells him to make himself at home. "Thanks," says the other, "I never stand on ceremony with my friends. That's how I understand hospitality." Maupassant continues: "Then he went upstairs, as he said, to dress as a farmer, and he came back all togged out in blue, with a little straw hat and yellow shoes. . . . He also seemed to become more vulgar, more jovial, more familiar, having put on with his country clothes a free and easy manner which he judged suitable for the occasion" (68).

15 In Latin America just the opposite obtains: one uses *tú* instead of *usted* in order to mark the familiarity of the new relationship. Brain is not clear about whether these practices are universal in Spain and Latin America or whether they are limited to Alcalá in Spain and Chinautleco in Guatemala. See Brain 99-101. The point, in any case, is not that only the formal (*usted*) can express intimacy, but that the informal (*tú*) has no privileged claim to it, contrary to our popular assumptions.

16 Cf. Elie Wiesel's *The Gates of the Forest,* in which the exchange of names between Gregor and Gavriel takes on the widest significance in terms of their friendship and a dozen other central themes in the novel.

17 Though he originally published it in *Notebook* (50), Lowell

revised this sonnet, including the ending, which I quote, and published it in *History* (126) as "Randall Jarrell: I. October 1965." The original version seems to me superior but Lowell did retain the invocation of the name in the revision:

> Randall, the scene still plunges at the windshield,
> apples redden to ripeness on the whiplash bough.

18 Simone de Beauvoir's formulation in 1952 has been very influential: "Women are comrades in captivity for one another, they help one another endure their prison, even help one another prepare for escape" (545–46). Also see Bernikow, Chesler, Lindsey, Smith-Rosenberg, and Strouse.

19 In this regard, the dominant concern of sociologists and anthropologists who have studied friendship has been its relation to kinship and social roles. See, for example, Allen, Bell, and the essays collected in Leyton.

20 Cf. the famous wrestling match of Birkin and Gerald in D. H. Lawrence's *Women in Love*.

21 Inviting a friend over for coffee seems to be a residue of the institution of the tea party.

22 It is hard to imagine a writer like Phyllis Chesler appreciating this scene in *The Sun Also Rises*. For her, "male bonding" is "the containment of explosive and crippling male rivalries, the systematic containment of indiscriminate acts of male violence. . . . Men 'bond' only temporarily, to avoid, or to commit, savage acts of betrayal or humiliation of other men" (241, 243). Lionel Tiger, whose view of male bonding is considerably less severe, though equally dubious, claims that "an aspect of male-bonding is its anti-femaleness," a feature also found "in the primates and in cultures differing enormously from each other in many fundamental respects." Far from being a conspiracy against women, he claims, this—like all other aspects of male bonding—is "as explicitly biological as the reproductive encounter" (48, 45, 44).

23 Cf. Brain, who on the basis of his extensive cross-cultural studies, concludes: "Very few of the examples of friendship and love between members of the same sex have any overt homoerotic element and in some instances it is actually taboo. . . . It is . . . silly to assume that physical contact is in itself evidence of homosexuality" (65).

24 Cf. John Boswell:

> In an intellectual tradition characterized by polarizing logic and mutually exclusive categories, failure to distinguish clearly between these areas of human emotion may seem quite serious, but from the scholar's point of view, any distinction between "friendship" and "love" must be extremely arbitrary. No scientific differentiation has ever

been proposed, nor is it easy to conceive of an experiment which might be performed to determine whether one person's love for another was friendly or erotic. From a phenomenological point of view, it seems likely that "friendship" and "love" are simply different points on a scale measuring a constellation of psychological and physiological responses to other humans.

From a historical point of view, the task of effecting such a division seems almost hopeless, since there is confusion and doubt not only in the historian's own frame of reference but also in that of the sources he uses. (46)

25 In her biography of Alice James, Jean Strouse quotes and discusses some letters of this kind, written by Alice James to Fanny Morse, among others. See 97–101, 183–84, and passim.

26 "While closeness, freedom of emotional expression, and uninhibited physical contact characterized women's relationships with each other," says Smith-Rosenberg, "the opposite was frequently true of male-female relationships" (27–28).

27 See Rosemary Rader, who argues that nonsexual male-female friendships were both numerous and important in early Christian communities; and Karen Lindsey, who makes the same point about contemporary American culture. For Lindsey, the family is the central model for nearly all aspects of friendship.

28 Justin Kaplan, in his recent biography, says that the *Calamus* poems constitute for Whitman an "act of self-exploration and in the end a recognition of his homosexuality at least as desire if not fulfillment" (236).

29 The word *comrades* recurs throughout Whitman's poetry, e.g., the final lines of section 6 of "Starting from Paumanok":

I will write the evangel-poem of comrades and of love,
For who but I should understand love with all its sorrow
    and joy?
And who but I should be the poet of comrades?

30 Rader discusses the early Christian practice of *syneisaktism* or celibate cohabitation, a kind of spiritual, sexless marriage between men and women devoted to Christian asceticism (62–71).

31 Brain points out that blood brotherhood is mentioned in Norse and Irish sagas and that "Herodotus mentions it for the Scythians and also for the Medes and Persians" (76).

2 Friendship as Gift Exchange

1 In my summary of Hyde's argument I also quote from his earlier article, "Some Food We Could Not Eat," which in some cases provides the best formulations of his central ideas. Hyde is not, of course, the first to have seen the importance of gift exchange; Lévi-Strauss, Mauss, and Sahlins (to take only

2 This organic quality of the gift is beautifully represented by an image in Sarah Orne Jewett's story "Martha's Lady" of a present given to Martha by her friend Helena. This "handkerchief with . . . narrow lace edge" Martha "once in two or three years . . . sprinkled as if it were a flower, and spread it out in the sun on the old bleaching-green, and sat nearby in the shrubbery to watch lest some bold robin or cherry-bird should seize it and fly away" (160). Cf. Nietzsche: "What regard we as the bad and worst thing? Is it not *degeneration?*— And we always suspect degeneration wherever the giving soul is lacking" (*Human* 103). Earlier Nietzsche says, "Gold-like shineth the glance of him who giveth," and he claims that "a giving virtue is the highest virtue," and that it is "of little use" (*Human* 102). Giving, for Nietzsche, is thus contrasted, as it is for Hyde, with the utilitarian.

3 Molière's *The Misanthrope* is the supreme example of a literary work that uses the language of economic exchange to explore human relations. In these terms one could, for example, talk about "investing" in a friendship or about a friendship becoming "inflated." For three short stories that make explicit use of the language of gift and economics in regard to friendship, see O. Henry, Shaw, and Van Doren. Cf. Plutarch, "Flatterer" (345).

4 Cf. Reynolds and especially Henry Miller, who recalls this fascinating episode from his childhood:

> I was embarrassed and ashamed that I should have everything I wanted while my companions lacked all but the bare necessities. One by one I gave my toys away to those who craved them. When I finally gave away the beautiful drum my parents had given me for my birthday I was severely punished. More than that, I was deeply humiliated. My mother had taken it into her head to recover some of the beautiful toys I had given away. So what did she do? She took me by the ear and dragged me to my friends' homes and made me ask for my toys back. She said that would teach me not to give away my presents. When I was old enough to buy my own things I could then give away whatever I chose. Presents cost money, I was to remember that. I did indeed remember her words, but not in the way she intended (2).

5 Brain also observes that the expense account "oils the wheels of business by allowing potentially inimical individuals to form friendship bonds through the symbolic process of sharing food.

[Afterwards], it is no longer pure business.... the friendship makes it less painful for George to exploit Bill" (145–46). One could as easily argue that the friendship would make the exploitation more painful. Cf. John D. Rockefeller's remark that "a friendship founded on business is better than a business founded on friendship" (Burke 2:40).

6 Jean Baker Miller argues that giving generally is more important to women than to men, who, she claims, value doing instead and often consider giving a luxury (49). That giving is so important for women she considers a mixed blessing.

7 Cf. the more complex proverb: "Make not thy friend too cheap to thee nor thyself too dear to him" (qtd. in Tilley 244).

8 Compare Diogenes' statement that "a friend's hand is open" (Davenport 47) and Ambrose Bierce's satirical quip: "While your friend holds you affectionately by both your hands you are safe, for you can watch both his" (qtd. in Mencken 435).

9 A colleague of mine tells me that his oldest, closest friend always keeps score, is fanatical about reciprocating, and is forever anxious that he has not adequately "paid back" his friend's kindness. This is an unusual situation, one more likely to be found in the initial stages of a friendship when one is trying to establish that the good feeling is mutual, or, in the case of an insecure partner, when one is anxious to prove that one is not exploiting the other. But though some of the spirit of gift is distorted here, it seems to me that this is just a surface obsession; after all, the man is not keeping score because he feels slighted—on the contrary.

10 Near the ending of Toni Morrison's *Sula,* the title character thinks about her old friend Nel, who has just left after visiting Sula on her deathbed. Nel had been bitter because Sula had seduced her husband. "So she will walk on down that road," Sula muses, "thinking how much I have cost her and never remember the days when we were two throats and one eye and we had no price" (126).

11 Aristotle also says that "each partner receives in all matters what he gives the others, in the same or in a similar form; that is what friends should be able to count on" (221). The language of gift and exchange recurs throughout Aristotle's discussion of friendship. See, for example, 258 f.

12 For a related but different perspective on generosity and gratitude, see Plutarch, "Flatterer" (337–41).

13 The distinction between commodity and gift exchange is implicit in numerous passages of *Cranford,* especially the section where the narrator is discussing Miss Matty's poverty and the candle-lighters, spills, and knitting-garters that she makes as "well-known tokens of [her] favour. But," the narrator asks, "would Miss Matty sell, for filthy lucre, the knack and skill

with which she made trifles of value to those who loved her?" 185–86).

14 For a discussion of the tradition of friendship continuing after death, see Mulder (165–66).
15 In these terms, aesthetic distance is in fact a means to closeness.
16 Cited in *Newsweek* 94 (17 September 1979):68.
17 Though La Rochefoucauld regarded friendship, like all other social relations, as a commercial transaction, he still considered true friendship extraordinary. See Keohane (292), who in this connection quotes maxim 473: "However rare true love may be, it is less rare than true friendship."
18 Cf. Robert Southwell's poem "A Childe My Choyse," which in line 8 refers to God: "First frende He was, best frende He is."
19 Bacon also refers to the Roman Senate dedicating "an altar to Friendship as to a goddess, in respect of the great dearness of friendship" between Tiberius Caesar and Sejanus (77–78).
20 Cf. Lepp: "Clare and Francis of Assissi, Teresa of Avila and John of the Cross, Jeanne de Chantal and Francis de Sales realized such great things for the glory of God at least partially because of their friendships. That such friendships are very much in keeping with the Christian spirit is proved by the fact that they were lauded by early hagiographers" (79). Lepp also tells us that "St. Anthony, who is taken to be the most austere of the desert fathers and whose ascetic practises strike us as excessive, left the desert only because of friendship. His friend Athanasius, bishop of Alexandria, was suffering persecution and Anthony hastened to lend him assistance" (25).
21 Though he does not discuss friendship, Foucault takes up the numerous respects in which confession has been secularized (58–73).
22 Cf. Keats's reference to "the wine of love—and the Bread of Friendship" (1.283). The *OED* indicates that the etymology of the word *companion* is *com* (together) *panis* (bread).
23 The same point applies to love. Cf. de Rougemont.
24 Erik Erikson quotes this prayer, called "Instrument of Thy Peace," and then adds: "Such commitment to initiative in love is, of course, contained in the admonition to 'love thy neighbor.' I think that we can recognize in these words a psychological verity, namely, that only he who approaches an encounter in a (consciously and unconsciously) active and giving attitude, rather than in a demanding and dependent one, will be able to make of that encounter what it can become" (232–33). The logic is of course similar to that of other spiritual paradoxes, e.g., Luke 17:33: "Whosoever shall seek to save his life shall lose it; and whosoever shall lose his life shall preserve it."

25 On the matter of preference, cf. C. S. Lewis, who claims that "the pride of Friendship—whether Olympian, Titanic, or merely vulgar— . . . is indeed almost inseparable from friendly love. Friendship must exclude. From the innocent and necessary act of excluding to the spirit of exclusiveness is an easy step; and thence to the degrading pleasure of exclusiveness" (101).

26 Cf. Graham Allen: "Friends can quite legitimately make use of one another in instrumental ways without threatening the relationship, provided that it is clear that they are being used because they are friends and not friends because they are useful. . . . It is so that friendships can be seen as nonexploitive that the ideas of reciprocity and symmetry are so important to them" (43–44).

3 *The Merchant of Venice*

1 See, for example, Auden ("Brothers and Others"), Bloom, Fiedler, Midgley, and Tovey. There is a lengthy proverbial literature warning against mixing friendship and money. For example: "Money makes friends enemies." "Even reckoning makes long friends." "He that sells upon trust loses many friends and always wants money." "Merchandise will have neither friends nor kindred" (qtd. in Tilley 469, 567, 684, 457). "No friendship in trade" (qtd. in Whiting 169). "Friendship is to be purchased only by friendship" (qtd. in Davidoff 160). Benjamin Nelson notes that "Antonio's suretyship for the debt of Bassanio has the flavor of a romantic archaism when set in contrast to the shrewd maxims of contemporary businessmen and statesmen" (147). He then cites examples from John Lyly, Lord Burghley, and Sir Walter Raleigh in which sons are warned by their fathers of the dangers of suretyship, even for friends (147–48). Still, according to Nelson, "the surety-hostage theme is integral to all the principal ancient and medieval friendship stories" (143n). Mark Twain's quip is characteristic both of him and of this long proverbial tradition: "The holy passion of Friendship is of so sweet and steady and loyal and enduring a nature that it will last through a whole lifetime if not asked to lend money" (33).

2 On the pervasive concern during the Renaissance with the more general theme of conflict between friendship and love, see Mills.

3 In a much more general context, not specifically related to *The Merchant of Venice,* Lynda E. Boose touches on some of the connections between gift exchange and marriage in Shakespeare's plays, and in the process she refers to the anthropological theories of, among others, Claude Lévi-Strauss and

Marcel Mauss (327, 329, 344). She does briefly discuss *The Merchant of Venice* in this article but not in terms of gift exchange (335–38).

4   Antonio has arranged to take the half of Shylock's wealth destined for himself and set it up in trust for Jessica and Lorenzo. In one sense Antonio is giving a gift to Jessica and Lorenzo as well.

5   It has been on similar grounds that many critics have seen the Christians in the play as hypocritical, especially because they fail to express agape for Shylock (Antonio has spit on him before and admits he might well do so again) and because they practice slavery. Meilaender does not refer to *The Merchant of Venice* but he observes that "the ideal of civic friendship in the polis was quite compatible with—probably dependent upon—a system of slavery. It may be that when some devote themselves to 'living well' others may be forced to deal solely with the needs of survival" (84). In these terms, Christianity's concern with universal brotherhood has not, in this play, altered the compatibility or dependence.

6   John Russell Brown, in *Shakespeare and His Comedies,* makes a similar point about "love as a kind of usury," arguing that whereas "Shylock practices a usury for the sake of gain and is prepared to enforce his rights; the lovers practice their usury without compulsion, for the joy of giving. . . . The comparison of the two usuries is part of a more general comparison of commerce and love" (64–65). For Brown, then, usury of commerce stands opposed to usury of love in a manner similar to the opposition I have drawn between commodity and gift exchange.

7   Marc Shell suggests that there is still another kind of spiritual usury in the play: " 'Spiritual usury,' say the church fathers, refers to hoping for gratitude, or some other kind of binding obligation, in return for giving a loan that is otherwise given gratis. Perhaps Antonio's loan of his body for Bassanio's wealth not only bound, but was also made with the intention of binding, Bassanio to him" (75).

8   Though Ann Barton distorts the issue by claiming that Portia forces Bassanio to recognize the conflict between her and Antonio, she does, finally, offer a convincing formulation of the resolution. The new relationship between Portia and Bassanio, she says, "although it does not cancel out friendship, relegates it, nonetheless, to a subordinate place. There is room for friendship within the house of love, but love holds the upper and controlling hand." That "hand, however, is Portia's and it is characteristically generous and full of gifts" (253).

9   Nerissa does not actually hand it to him but it is clear that when Portia says to Lorenzo, "My clerk hath some good com-

forts too for you" (5.1.289), she has in mind the ring in addition to the more obvious sexual implications. "Ay," says Nerissa, "and I'll give them him without a fee" (5.1.290). By this point, the rings have become so sexually symbolic that the distinction collapses.

10 Meilaender addresses only the general political issue but his conclusion seems applicable as a description of Shakespeare's position in *The Merchant of Venice:* "The truth, rather—and the best we can and should hope for—is that justice in the political order should nourish and foster private friendships. That is not a self-regarding goal, even if it settles for something less universal than civic friendship; for private friendships, though not universal in scope, are genuinely other-regarding" (75).

11 Arthur Kirsch, on the contrary, suggests that Shakespeare dwells on Antonio's sense of loss and sadness to suggest not that Antonio's love for Bassanio is masochistic or homosexual but to show the pain of self-denial (41). Though Kirsch has in mind a more general and spiritual self-denial, he need not oppose that to homosexuality; one can, indeed, grant a certain homosexual impulse and consider its repression another—if more physical and psychological—form of self-denial. For a very different view of Antonio's sadness, see René Girard.

12 In these terms, Antonio's pound of flesh becomes an almost literal example of giving a part of one's substance.

13 The rewards are also great for Antonio, whose ships now come in. That metaphor—of one's ship coming in—contributes to our sense that we need not be too literal in interpreting Portia's good news for Antonio. One objection to my claim that Portia is giving Antonio a disguised gift would be that one need not find such a specific explanation for a turn of events that is consistent with the comic convention of happy resolutions. But the point is moot, because such an appeal would equally discredit the charge that I am not being literal enough.

14 After he says this, Jesus refers to his followers as friends rather than servants, and of course he does, in one sense, lay down his life for his friends.

Works Cited

Abrahams, Roger D. *Deep Down in the Jungle: Negro Narrative Folklore from the Streets of Philadelphia.* 1963. Chicago: Aldine, 1970.
Adams, Henry. *The Education of Henry Adams.* 1918. Sentry ed. Boston: Houghton, 1961.
Allen, Graham A. *A Sociology of Friendship and Kinship.* London: George Allen and Unwin, 1979.
Anderson, Jon. *Death & Friends.* Pittsburgh: U of Pittsburgh P, 1970.
Aristotle. *Nicomachean Ethics.* Trans. Martin Oswald. Indianapolis: Bobbs-Merrill, 1962.
Auden, W. H. *About the House.* New York: Random House, 1965.
———. "Brothers and Others." In *The Dyer's Hand and Other Essays.* New York: Random House, 1962, 218–37.
Auden, W. H., and Louis Kronenberger, eds. *The Viking Book of Aphorisms.* New York: Viking, 1963.
Augustine, St. *The Confessions of St. Augustine.* Trans. Edward B. Pusey. New York: Modern Library–Random, 1949.
Austen, Jane. *Love and Friendship.* In *Volume the Second.* Ed. B. C. Southam. Oxford: Clarendon, 1963, 3–66.
Bacon, Francis. "Of Friendship." In *Essays, Advancement of Learning, New Atlantis, and Other Pieces.* Ed. Richard Foster Jones. New York: Odyssey, 1937, 75–82.
Barber, C. L. *Shakespeare's Festive Comedy: A Study of Dramatic Form and its Relation to Social Custom.* Princeton: Princeton UP, 1959.
Bartlett, John. *Familiar Quotations.* 15th ed. Ed. Emily Morrison Beck. Boston: Little, 1980.
Barton, Ann. Introduction. *The Merchant of Venice.* In *The Riverside Shakespeare.* Ed. G. Blakemore Evans et al. Boston: Houghton, 1974, 250–53.

Beauvoir, Simone de. *The Second Sex*. Trans. and ed. H. M. Parshley. 1952. New York: Knopf, 1976.
Bell, Robert R. *Worlds of Friendship*. Sociological Observations Series. Beverly Hills: Sage, 1981.
Benston, Alice N. "Portia, the Law, and the Tripartite Structure of *The Merchant of Venice*." *Shakespeare Quarterly* 30 (1979): 367-85.
Bergson, Henri. "Laughter." In *Comedy*. Ed. Wylie Sypher. Garden City, NY: Anchor-Doubleday, 1956, 61-190.
Bernikow, Louise. *Among Women*. New York: Harmony, 1980.
Blake, William. *The Complete Poetry and Prose of William Blake*. Rev. ed. Ed. David V. Erdman. Berkeley: U of California P, 1982.
Bloom, Allan. "On Christian and Jew." In *Shakespeare's Politics*. By Allan Bloom and Harry Jaffa. New York: Basic, 1964, 13-34.
Blum, Lawrence. *Friendship, Altruism and Morality*. London: Routledge & Kegan Paul, 1980.
Boose, Lynda E. "The Father and the Bride in Shakespeare." *PMLA* 97 (1982): 325-47.
Booth, Wayne C. " 'The Way I Loved George Eliot': Friendship with Books as a Neglected Critical Metaphor." *Kenyon Review*, n.s. 2 (1980): 4-27.
Boswell, James. *Life of Johnson*. 2d ed. Ed. R. W. Chapman. Oxford Standard Authors. London: Oxford UP, 1953.
Boswell, John. *Christianity, Social Tolerance, and Homosexuality: Gay People in Western Europe from the Beginning of the Christian Era to the Fourteenth Century*. Chicago: U of Chicago P, 1980.
Brain, Robert. *Friends and Lovers*. New York: Basic, 1976.
Brodsky, Joseph. *A Part of Speech*. New York: Farrar, Straus & Giroux, 1980.
Brown, John Russell. Introduction. *The Arden Edition of The Merchant of Venice*. By William Shakespeare. Ed. John Russell Brown. London: Methuen, 1955, xi-lviii.
———. *Shakespeare and His Comedies*. 2nd ed. London: Methuen, 1962.
Bry, Adelaide. *Friendship: How to Have a Friend and Be a Friend*. New York: Grosset and Dunlap, 1979.
Burke, John Gordon, Deborah Davis, Ned Kehde, and Jill Swanson Reddig, eds. *Dictionary of Contemporary Quotations*. Gaylord Professional Publications. Syracuse, NY: John Gordon Burke, 1976. Vol. 2.
Burke, Kenneth. Letter to author. 18 June 1980.
Butler, Samuel. *The Way of All Flesh*. 1903. New York: Dutton, 1916.

Camus, Albert. *The Stranger.* Trans. Stuart Gilbert. 1946. New York: Vintage-Random, 1954.

Carpenter, Edward, ed. *Ioläus: An Anthology of Friendship.* London: Swan Sonnenschein, 1902.

Chesler, Phyllis. *About Men.* New York: Simon and Schuster, 1978.

Cicero. "On Friendship." In *On Old Age and On Friendship.* Trans. Frank O. Copley. 1967. Ann Arbor: U of Michigan P, 1971, 43–90.

Danson, Lawrence. *The Harmonies of the Merchant of Venice.* New Haven: Yale UP, 1978.

Davenport, Guy, trans. *Herakleitos and Diogenes.* Bolinas, CA: Grey Fox, 1979.

Davidoff, Henry, ed. *A World Treasury of Proverbs from Twenty-five Languages.* New York: Random House, 1946.

Dickinson, Emily. *The Poems of Emily Dickinson.* Ed. Thomas H. Johnson. 3 vols. Cambridge, MA: Belknap Press, Harvard UP, 1955.

Donne, John. *Poetical Works.* Ed. Sir Herbert Grierson. 1933. Oxford: Oxford UP, 1977.

Dryden, John. *The Works of John Dryden.* Vol. 3: *Poems 1685–1692.* Ed. Earl Miner et al. Berkeley: U of California P, 1969.

Du Bois, Cora. "The Gratuitous Act: An Introduction to the Comparative Study of Friendship Patterns." In *The Compact: Selected Dimensions of Friendship.* Ed. Elliott Leyton. Newfoundland Social and Economic Papers, no. 3. Toronto: U of Toronto P, 1974, 15–32.

Eliot, T. S. "The Love Song of J. Alfred Prufrock." In *Collected Poems: 1909–1962.* New York: Harcourt, 1963, 3–7.

Emerson, Ralph Waldo. "Friendship." In *The Collected Works of Ralph Waldo Emerson.* Vol. 2: *Essays: First Series.* Ed. Joseph Slater, Alfred R. Ferguson, and Jean Ferguson Carr. Cambridge, MA: Belknap-Harvard UP, 1979, 111–27.

―――. *The Journals and Miscellaneous Notebooks of Ralph Waldo Emerson.* Vol. 1. Ed. A. W. Plumstead and Harrison Hayford. Cambridge, MA: Harvard UP, 1969.

Erikson, Erik H. *Insight and Responsibility: Lectures on the Ethical Implications of Psychoanalytic Insight.* New York: Norton, 1964.

Fiedler, Leslie. *The Stranger in Shakespeare.* New York: Stein and Day, 1972.

Fielding, Henry. *The Works of Henry Fielding.* Vol. 8: *Amelia.* Ed. G. H. Maynadier. New York: George D. Sproul, 1903.

Fiske, Adele M. *Friends and Friendship in the Monastic Tradition.* Cidoc Cuaderno, no. 51. Cuernavaca, Mexico, 1970.

Fitzgerald, F. Scott. *The Notebooks of F. Scott Fitzgerald.* Ed. Matthew Bruccoli. New York: Harcourt, 1978.

Forster, E. M. *The Abinger Edition of E. M. Forster.* Ed. Oliver Stallybrass. Vol. 6: *A Passage to India.* New York: Holmes and Meier, 1979.
———. "What I Believe." In *The Abinger Edition of E. M. Forster.* Ed. Oliver Stallybrass. Vol. 11: *Two Cheers for Democracy.* London: Edward Arnold, 1972, 65–73.
Foucault, Michel. *The History of Sexuality.* Vol. 1: *An Introduction.* Trans. Robert Hurley. 1978. New York: Vintage-Random, 1980.
Gaskell, Elizabeth. *Cranford/Cousin Phillis.* Ed. Peter Keating. Harmondsworth, Eng.: Penguin, 1976.
Girard, René. " 'To Entrap the Wisest': A Reading of *The Merchant of Venice.*" In *Literature and Society: Selected Papers from the English Institute, 1978.* Ed. Edward W. Said. Baltimore: Johns Hopkins UP, 1980, 100–119.
Gluski, Jerzy, ed. *Proverbs: A Comparative Book of English, French, German, Italian, Spanish, and Russian Proverbs, with a Latin Appendix.* Amsterdam: Elsevier, 1971.
Goethe, Johann Wolfgang von. *Torquato Tasso.* In *Goethe's Plays.* Trans. Charles E. Passage. New York: Frederick Ungar, 1980, 483–592.
Goldbarth, Albert. "Thish Beélya." *Carolina Quarterly* 34 (1981): 53–58.
Greeley, Andrew M. *The Friendship Game.* Garden City, NY: Doubleday, 1970.
Guterman, Norbert, ed. *A Book of French Quotations with English Translations.* Garden City, NY: Doubleday, 1963.
Hans, James S. *The Play of the World.* Amherst: U of Massachusetts P, 1981.
Hartrup, Willard W. "The Origins of Friendship." In *Friendship and Peer Relations.* Ed. Michael Lewis and Leonard A. Rosenblum. New York: Wiley, 1975, 11–26.
Hecht, Anthony. *The Hard Hours: Poems.* New York: Atheneum, 1968.
Hellman, Lillian. "Julia." In *Pentimento.* 1973. New York: Signet, 1974, 81–121.
Hemingway, Ernest. *The Sun Also Rises.* 1926. New York: Scribner's, 1970.
Henderson, Bill, ed. *The Pushcart Prize, VI: Best of the Small Presses, 1979–80.* Yonkers, NY: Pushcart, 1979.
Henry, O. "Friends in San Rosario." In *The Complete Works of O. Henry.* Special Literary Digest Edition. New York: Doubleday, 1926, 352–59.
Holland, Lady Saba. *A Memoir of the Reverend Sydney Smith.* Ed. Mrs. Austin. Vol. 1. 4th ed. London: Longman, 1855.
Hutter, Horst. *Politics as Friendship: The Origins of Classical No-*

tions of Politics in the Theory and Practise of Friendship. Waterloo, Can.: Wilfred Laurier UP, 1978.
Hyde, Lewis. *The Gift: Imagination and the Erotic Life of Property.* New York: Random, 1983.
———. "Some Food We Could Not Eat: Gift Exchange and the Imagination." *Kenyon Review,* n.s. 1 (1979): 32–60.
Ibsen, Henrik. *Love's Comedy.* Trans. C. H. Herford. London: Duckworth, 1900.
Irving, John. "In Defense of Sentimentality." *New York Times Book Review* 129 (25 November 1979): 3, 96.
Jewett, Sarah Orne. "Martha's Lady." In *The Queen's Twin and Other Stories.* 1899. Short Story Index Reprint Series. Freeport, NY: Books for Libraries Press, 1971, 135–69.
Johnson, Samuel. "Rambler 64." In *The Yale Edition of the Works of Samuel Johnson.* Vol. 3: *The Rambler.* Ed. W. J. Bate and Albrecht B. Strauss. New Haven: Yale UP, 1969, 339–44.
Kafka, Franz. *The Metamorphosis.* In *The Penal Colony: Stories and Short Pieces.* Trans. Willa and Edwin Muir. New York: Schocken, 1948, 67–132.
Kaplan, Justin. *Walt Whitman: A Life.* New York: Simon and Schuster, 1980.
Keats, John. *The Letters of John Keats: 1814–1821.* Ed. Hyder Edward Rollins. 2 vols. Cambridge, MA: Harvard UP, 1958.
Keohane, Nannerl O. *Philosophy and the State in France: The Renaissance to the Enlightenment.* Princeton: Princeton UP, 1980.
Kirsch, Arthur. Unpublished and untitled paper on *The Merchant of Venice.* 1973.
Knowles, John. *A Separate Peace.* New York: Delta-Dell, 1959.
Lai, T. C. *A Chinese Book of Friendship.* Kow Loon, Hong Kong: Swindon, 1973.
Lamb, Charles. "A Bachelor's Complaint of the Behaviour of Married People." In *The Library Edition of the Life and Works of Charles Lamb.* Vol. 2: *The Essays of Elia.* Ed. Alfred Ainger. Troy, NY: Pafraets, 1902, 246–56.
Lawrence, D. H. *Women in Love.* Ed. Charles Ross. Harmondsworth, Eng.: Penguin, 1982.
Lee, Susan. "Friendship, Feminism, and Betrayal." *The Village Voice* (1975). Rpt. *The Norton Reader: An Anthology of Expository Prose.* 4th ed. Ed. Arthur M. Eastman et al. New York: Norton, 1977, 589–95.
Lepp, Ignace. *The Ways of Friendship.* Trans. Bernard Murchland. 1966. New York: Macmillan, 1968.
Lévi-Strauss, Claude. *The Elementary Structures of Kinship.* Trans. James Bell, John Richard von Sturmer, and Rodney Needham. Boston: Beacon Press, 1969.
Lewis, C. S. *The Four Loves.* London: Geoffrey Bles, 1960.

Lewis, Michael, and Leonard A. Rosenblum, eds. *Friendship and Peer Relations.* New York: Wiley, 1975.
Leyton, Elliott, ed. *The Compact: Selected Dimensions of Friendship.* Newfoundland Social and Economic Papers, no. 3. Toronto: U of Toronto P, 1974.
Lindsey, Karen. *Friends as Family.* Boston: Beacon Press, 1981.
London, Jack. *South Sea Tales.* Cleveland: World, 1946.
Lowell, Robert. *History.* New York: Farrar, Straus & Giroux, 1973.
———. *Life Studies.* New York: Farrar, Straus & Cudahy, 1959.
———. *Notebook.* New York: Farrar, Straus & Giroux, 1970.
Malory, Sir Thomas. *The Works of Sir Thomas Malory.* 2nd ed. Ed. Eugene Vinaver. Oxford: Clarendon, 1967.
Malraux, André. *Man's Fate.* Trans. Haakon M. Chevalier. New York: Modern Library–Random, 1934.
———. *Man's Hope.* Trans. Stuart Gilbert and Alastair Macdonald. New York: Modern Library–Random, 1941.
Martial. *Epigrams.* Trans. Walter C. A. Kerr. 1919. Loeb Classical Library. Ed. T. E. Page. London: William Heinemann, 1930.
Martin, Robert K. *The Homosexual Tradition in American Poetry.* Austin: U of Texas P, 1979.
Maupassant, Guy de. "Friend Joseph." In *The Complete Works of de Maupassant.* Trans. Alfred de Sumichrast et al. Vol. 1: *The Window and Short Stories.* Boston: C. T. Brainard, 1910, 65–71.
Mauss, Marcel. *The Gift: Forms and Functions of Exchanges in Archaic Societies.* Trans. Ian Cunnison. New York: Norton, 1967.
Mead, Frank S., ed. *The Encyclopedia of Religious Quotations.* Westwood, NJ: Fleming H. Revell, 1965.
Meilaender, Gilbert C. *Friendship: A Study in Theological Ethics.* Notre Dame, IN: U of Notre Dame P, 1981.
Mencken, H. L., ed. *A New Dictionary of Quotations.* New York: Knopf, 1942.
Midgley, Graham. "*The Merchant of Venice* A Reconsideration." In *"The Merchant of Venice": A Casebook.* Ed. John Wilders. London: Macmillan, 1969, 193–207.
Mill, John Stuart. *Autobiography.* In *The Collected Works of John Stuart Mill.* Vol. 1: *Autobiography and Literary Essays.* Ed. John M. Robson and Jack Stillinger. Toronto: U of Toronto P, 1981, 1–290.
Miller, Henry. *The Book of Friends: A Tribute to Friends of Long Ago.* Santa Barbara, CA: Capra, 1976.
Miller, Jean Baker. *Toward a New Psychology of Women.* Boston: Beacon Press, 1976.
Mills, Laurens J. *One Soul in Bodies Twain: Friendship in Tudor Literature and Stuart Drama.* Bloomington: Indiana UP, 1937.

Milton, John. *Complete Poems and Major Prose.* Ed. Merritt Y. Hughes. Indianapolis: Bobbs-Merrill, 1957.

Molière. *The Misanthrope.* Trans. Richard Wilbur. New York: Harcourt, 1955.

Montaigne, Michel de. "On Friendship." In *Essays.* Trans. J. M. Cohen. Harmondsworth, Eng.: Penguin, 1958, 91–105.

Morris, Colin. *The Discovery of the Individual: 1050–1200.* New York: Harper, 1972.

Morrison, Toni. *Sula.* 1973. New York: Bantam, 1975.

Mulder, Mab Lohuizen. *Raphael's Images of Justice—Humanity—Friendship: A Mirror of Princes for Scipione Borghese.* Trans. Patricia Wardle. Wassenaar, Neth.: Mirananda, 1977.

Myerhoff, Barbara. *Number Our Days.* 1978. New York: Simon and Schuster, 1980.

———. "A Renewal of the Word." *Kenyon Review,* n.s. 1 (1979): 50–79.

Nelson, Benjamin. *The Idea of Usury: From Tribal Brotherhood to Universal Otherhood.* 2nd ed. Chicago: U of Chicago P, 1969.

Nietzsche, Friedrich. *The Complete Works of Friedrich Nietzsche.* Ed. Oscar Levy. Vol. 6: *Human, All-Too-Human: A Book for Free Spirits.* Trans. Helen Zimmern. New York: Macmillan, 1924.

———. *The Complete Works of Friedrich Nietzsche.* Ed. Oscar Levy. Vol. 2: *Thus Spake Zarathustra: A Book for All and None.* Trans. Alexander Tille. New York: Macmillan, 1906.

Nin, Anaïs. *The Diary of Anaïs Nin.* Ed. Gunther Stuhlmann. Vol. 2. New York: Swallow and Harcourt, 1969.

Oates, Joyce Carol. "Love. Friendship." In *Crossing the Border: Fifteen Tales.* New York: Vanguard, 1976, 15–38.

Opie, Iona and Peter. *The Lore and Language of Schoolchildren.* Oxford: Clarendon, 1959.

Paine, Robert. "An Exploratory Analysis in 'Middle-Class' Culture." In *The Compact: Selected Dimensions of Friendship.* Ed. Elliot Leyton. Newfoundland Social and Economic Papers, no. 3. Toronto: U of Toronto P, 1974, 117–37.

Peter, Lawrence J. *Peter's Quotations: Ideas for Our Time.* New York: William Morrow, 1977.

Piercy, Marge. *Living in the Open: Poems.* New York: Knopf, 1976.

Plato. *The Collected Dialogues of Plato.* Ed. Edith Hamilton and Huntington Cairns. Bollingen Series, no. 71. New York: Pantheon, 1961.

Plutarch. "How To Tell a Flatterer from a Friend." In *Plutarch's Moralia.* Trans. Frank Cole Babbitt. Loeb Classical Library, vol. 1. London: William Heinemann, 1927, 261–395.

———. "On Having Many Friends." In *Plutarch's Moralia.* Trans.

Frank Cole Babbitt. Loeb Classical Library, vol. 2. London: William Heinemann, 1927, 43–69.

Pound, Ezra. *Personae: The Collected Shorter Poems.* 1926. New York: New Directions, 1949.

Racine, Jean. *Berenice.* In *The Complete Plays of Jean Racine.* Trans. Samuel Solomon. New York: Random House, 1967, 1: 373–444.

Rader, Rosemary. *Breaking Boundaries: Male/Female Friendship in Early Christian Communities.* New York: Paulist Press, 1983.

Reynolds, Vernon. "Friendship among the Primates." In *The Compact: Selected Dimensions of Friendship.* Ed. Elliott Leyton. Newfoundland Social and Economic Papers, no. 3. Toronto: U of Toronto P, 1974, 33–41.

Rich, Adrienne. *The Dream of a Common Language: Poems, 1974–1977.* New York: Norton, 1978.

———. *Poems: Selected and New, 1950–1974.* New York: Norton, 1975.

Rougemont, Denis de. *Love in the Western World.* Trans. Montgomery Belgion. Rev. ed. New York: Fawcett, 1956.

Roux, Joseph. *Meditations of a Parish Priest. Thoughts.* Translated from the 3d ed. by Isabel F. Mapgood. New York: T. Y. Crowell and Son, 1886.

Sahlins, Marshall. *Stone Age Economics.* Chicago: Aldine, 1972.

Salinger, J. D. *The Catcher in the Rye.* Boston: Little, Brown, 1951.

Santayana, George. "Friendship." In *The Birth of Reason and Other Essays.* Ed. Daniel Cory. New York: Columbia UP, 1968, 78–89.

Schiller, Friedrich. *On the Aesthetic Education of Man.* Trans. and ed. E. M. Wilkinson and L. A. Willoughby. Oxford: Clarendon, 1967.

Schultz, Philip. *Upstart Crows.* Forthcoming. (References are to manuscript pages).

Scott, Nathan A., Jr. *The Poetry of Civic Virtue: Eliot, Malraux, Auden.* Philadelphia: Fortress, 1976.

Selden, Elizabeth, ed. *The Book of Friendship: An International Anthology.* Boston: Houghton Mifflin, 1947.

Seneca. "De Beneficiis." Volume 3 of *Moral Essays.* Trans. John W. Basore. Loeb Classical Library. London: William Heinemann, 1935.

Shakespeare, William. *First Part of Henry IV.* 6th Arden ed. Ed. A. R. Humphreys. London: Methuen, 1960.

———. *Hamlet.* Arden ed. Ed. Harold Jenkins. London: Methuen, 1982.

———. *King Lear.* 8th Arden ed. Ed. Kenneth Muir. London: Methuen, 1957.

———. *The Merchant of Venice*. 7th Arden ed. rev. Ed. John Russell Brown. London: Methuen, 1955.
———. *The Taming of the Shrew*. Arden ed. Ed. Brian Morris. London: Methuen, 1981.
Shaw, Irwin. "Act of Faith." In *Short Stories: Five Decades*. New York: Delacorte, 1978, 243–56.
Shell, Marc. *Money, Language, and Thought: Literary and Philosophical Economies from the Medieval to the Modern Era*. Berkeley: U of California P, 1982.
Smith-Rosenberg, Carroll. "The Female World of Love and Ritual: Relations between Women in Nineteenth Century America." *Signs* 1 (1975): 1–29.
Solzhenitsyn, Aleksandr. *The Oak and the Calf: Memoirs of a Literary Life*. Trans. Harry Willetts. New York: Harper, 1980.
Sophocles. *Antigone*. Trans. Elizabeth Wyckoff. In *The Complete Greek Tragedies*. Ed. David Grene and Richmond Lattimore. Vol. 1: *Sophocles*. Chicago: U of Chicago P, 1954, 157–204.
Southwell, Robert. *Complete Poems of Robert Southwell*. Ed. Alexander B. Grosart. 1872. New York: A.M.S., 1971.
Steiner, George. "Reflections: The Cleric of Treason." *The New Yorker* 56 (8 December 1980): 158–95.
Stevenson, Burton, ed. *The Home Book of Quotations: Classical and Modern*. 10th ed. New York: Dodd, 1967.
Stevenson, Robert Louis. *Travels With a Donkey*. In *The Vailima Edition of the Works of Robert Louis Stevenson*. Vol. 1. New York: Scribner's, 1921, 179–363.
Strouse, Jean. *Alice James: A Biography*. 1980. Toronto: Bantam, 1982.
Thoreau, Henry D. *The Writings of Henry D. Thoreau: A Week on the Concord and Merrimack Rivers*. Ed. Carl F. Hovde. Princeton: Princeton UP, 1980.
Tiger, Lionel. "Sex-Specific Friendship." In *The Compact: Selected Dimensions of Friendship*. Ed. Elliott Leyton. Newfoundland Social and Economic Papers, no. 3. Toronto: U of Toronto P, 1974, 42–48.
Tilley, Morris Palmer, ed. *A Dictionary of the Proverbs in England in the Sixteenth and Seventeenth Centuries*. Ann Arbor: U of Michigan P, 1950.
Tocqueville, Alexis de. *Democracy in America*. Vol. 2. Trans. Henry Reeve. Ed. Francis Bowen and Phillips Bradley. New York: Vintage-Random, 1954.
Tovey, Barbara. "The Golden Casket: An Interpretation of *The Merchant of Venice*." In *Shakespeare as Political Thinker*. Ed. John Alvis and Thomas G. West. Durham: Carolina Academic Press, 1981, 215–39.
Trilling, Lionel. *Sincerity and Authenticity*. Cambridge, MA: Harvard UP, 1972.

Twain, Mark. *Pudd'nhead Wilson.* In *The Norton Critical Edition of Samuel Langhorne Clemens' Pudd'nhead Wilson and Those Extraordinary Twins.* Ed. Sidney E. Berger. New York: Norton, 1980, 1–115.

Uhlman, Fred. *Reunion.* 1971. Harmondsworth, Eng.: Penguin, 1978.

Van Doren, Mark. "Some Friend." In *Collected Stories.* Vol. 1. New York: Hill and Wang, 1968, 134–44.

Walcott, Derek. *The Star-Apple Kingdom.* New York: Farrar, Straus and Giroux, 1979.

Whiting, Bartlett Jere, ed. *Early American Proverbs and Proverbial Phrases.* Cambridge, MA: Belknap-Harvard UP, 1977.

Whiting, Bartlett Jere, and Helen Wescott, eds. *Proverbs, Sentences, and Proverbial Phrases from English Writings Mainly before 1500.* Cambridge, MA: Belknap Press of Harvard UP, 1968.

Whitman, Walt. *The Collected Writings of Walt Whitman.* Vol. 9: *Leaves of Grass: Comprehensive Reader's Edition.* Ed. Harold W. Blodgett and Sculley Bradley. New York: New York UP, 1965.

———. "Poetry To-Day in America—Shakspere—The Future." *The Collected Writings of Walt Whitman.* Vol. 8: *Prose Works 1892.* Ed. Floyd Stovall. New York: New York UP, 1965, 474–90.

Wiesel, Elie. *The Gates of the Forest.* Trans. Frances Frenaye. 1966. New York: Schocken Books, 1982.

Wilde, Oscar. "The Critic as Artist." In *The Artist as Critic: Critical Writings of Oscar Wilde.* Ed. Richard Ellman. New York: Random, 1969, 340–408.

Wilson, Thomas. *A Discourse Upon Usury.* 1572. New York: Harcourt, 1925.

Wordsworth, William. *Poetical Works With Introduction and Notes.* Ed. Thomas Hutchinson. New ed. Rev. Ernest De Selincourt. Oxford Standard Authors. London: Oxford UP, 1969.

Index

Adams, Henry, 44
Adolescence: gift exchange in, 87; and rituals in friendship, 14–16
Adversity, sharing of, 44–45, 55
Aelred, Abbot, 111
Affection, expression of: by females, 64; by males, 63–64, 65–67, 156; vehicles for, 58–62
Aggression: in friendship, 54; latent sentiments of, 42–43, 45–46
Alienation and loneliness, 3–4; and functions of friendship, 114
Allen, Graham, 32, 163
Altruism, 52–53
Amusement in friendships, 38–39; and importance of jokes, 41–42
Anderson, Jon, 61, 62
Anselm, Saint, 111
Anthropological studies: of friendship, 2, 11–12, 77, 78; of gift giving, 97
Anxiety over friendships, 12, 24
Aristotle, 7, 32, 37, 44, 55, 87–88, 91, 92, 94, 95, 141, 142, 148, 161
Art: compared to play and games, 36–37; as gift, 103
Art of friendship, 29
Auden, W. H., 21–23, 135, 142, 163
Augustine, Saint, 102, 104
Austen, Jane, 49, 50–51, 54
Authenticity, ethic of, 25–26, 80–81
Authority, friendship as threat to, 157

Bacon, Francis, 38, 55, 112, 162
Balance or equilibrium in friendship, 89, 91
Barber, C. L., 126
Barton, Ann, 128, 164
Beauvoir, Simone de, 158
Benston, Alice N., 136–37, 141
Bergson, Henri, 39
Bernikow, Louise, 87
Biblical references: to friendship, 110, 112, 152, 165; to usury, 132
Bierce, Ambrose, 161
Blackstone, William, 132
Blake, William, 26, 40, 118

Blood brotherhood, 14, 78, 87, 159
Bloom, Allan, 131, 145, 163
Blum, Lawrence A., 53
Boose, Lynda E., 163–64
Booth, Wayne, 4
Boswell, James, 9, 37
Boswell, John, 71, 111, 158
Brain, Robert, 2, 11, 13, 24, 41–42, 43, 57, 68, 77, 78, 79, 87, 155, 157, 158, 159, 160
Brodsky, Joseph, 59, 61
Brotherhood: and blood brother concept, 14, 78, 87, 159; and bonds of community, 131–33
Brown, John Russell, 122, 125, 164
Bry, Adelaide, 50
Buddy relationships, 73–74
Burghley, Lord, 163
Burke, Kenneth, 8
Business activities, friendship in, 160–61
Butler, Samuel, 120

Camus, Albert, 3, 4
Carpenter, Edward, 58
Ceremony: aversion to, 12, 23; denial of, 24
Chamfort, Nicolas-Sébastien, 112
Chesler, Phyllis, 158
Children: gift exchange by, 86–87; rituals in friendship, 14
Chinautleco Indians, friendship among, 78
Cicero, 27, 37, 44, 53, 55, 88, 91, 92, 94, 100–103, 109
Closeness: effect of distance on, 56, 162
Co-godparenthood, 11, 78–79
Collections, sharing of, 15–16
Comfortable quality of friendship, 37–38
Comic features of friendship, 38–39; and importance of jokes, 41–42

Commodity or market exchange, compared to gifts, 84–86, 88, 161
Community: and concept of fraternity, 116; and friendship as threat to authority, 157; and issue of insiders and outsiders, 131–33
Compadrazgo, 78–79
Compassion: and emotional control, 49; and excessive generosity, 91–92; mercy and justice in, 135, 141–42; and self-interest, 52–53
Competition among friends, 43–44, 45–46, 54
Concealment of feelings: effect on friendship, 55–56
Confession: and friendship, 29, 162; in women's groups, 64
Conflict: between love and friendship, 164; in demands from numerous friends, 95–96
Congeniality in friendship, 37
Conventions: of confessional poetry, 29; and sentimentality, 50–51; and sexual roles, 143–44
Courting of friends, 14–15, 158
Creativity: and gift giving, 93; and use of forms, 13, 24, 51, 62, 79–80, 153–54
Crisis insurance: as function of friendship, 45, 46
Cultural aspects of friendship, 2, 11–12
Culture of friendship, 39–41; compared to larger cultures, 40–41
Cynical views of friendship, 5, 44, 54, 119–20, 146–47

Damon and Pythias, 110–11
Danson, Lawrence, 122
Dante, 41, 131, 143
Death: and continuance of friendship, 162; and immor-

tality through friendship,
    101–9
Dedications, expression of
    affection in, 59
Dickinson, Emily, 40
Dinners. *See* Meal sharing
Diogenes, 100, 161
Distance: and creation of closeness, 56, 162
Donne, John, 28
Douglas, Norman, 29
Dryden, John, 112
Du Bois, Cora, 120

Eating. *See* Meal sharing
Economic exchange: and language of gift giving, 160
Eliot, T. S., 3
Emerson, Ralph Waldo, 80, 112
Emotions: and compassion, 49; vehicles for expression of, 58–62
Encounter groups, ideology of, 25–26, 45
Enjoyment and congeniality in friendship, 37–38
Envy in friendship, 45
Equilibrium or balance in friendship, 89, 91
Erikson, Erik, 162
Erotic elements in friendship, 70–77
Excitement and relaxation in friendship, 37–38
Exclusiveness in friendship, 163
Exotic rituals in friendship, 11, 78

Family: as model for friendship, 159
Female friendships, 158, 159; affection expressed in, 64; gift exchange in, 87, 161
Female-male friendship, 73, 137, 159, 162
Fielding, Henry, 94, 112
Fiske, Adele M., 111

Fitzgerald, Scott, 112
Forms, 155–59; circumvention of, 28, 80; and creativity, 13, 24, 51, 62, 79–80, 153; denial and suspicion of, 24–25; and expression of affection, 58–62; as function in friendship, 9, 11–81; and gift giving, 153; and hospitality, 20–23; and meals as rituals, 19–22; opposition to, 13, 23–24; in parting of friends, 16–18; in reunion of friends, 18–20; and sincerity, 49. *See also* Ritual activities
Forster, E. M., 41, 93
Foucault, Michel, 155, 162
Francis of Assisi, 114, 162
Frankness. *See* Openness and frankness
Fraternity, concept of, 116
Freedom: and form, 23–24, 154; and obligations of friendship, 23–24; and obligations of marriage, 152

Games and play, 35–37; aggression and rivalry in, 42–43; insults in, 41–43, 157
Gaskell, Elizabeth, 46; and examples from *Cranford*, 46–49, 51–53, 54–56, 64, 88, 94–95, 161
Gender differences in friendship, 63–77
Generosity, excessive, 91–92
Gestures and language in friendships, 39–40
Giacometti, Alberto, 4
Gift giving, 9, 82–117, 159–63; and bonds of community, 131–33; and buying favor with friendship, 133, 146; as circular movement, 85, 98, 103, 108–9, 115, 130, 152; compared to commodity or market exchange, 84–86, 88,

Gift giving (*Cont.*)
161; cumulative effects of, 134–39; and friendships of women, 64; and idea of return, 85, 88–89, 114, 117; and immortality, 101–9; in *The Merchant of Venice*, 122–42; and need for reciprocation, 89, 161; negative aspects of, 86, 133–34; paradoxical logic in, 84–85, 94–95, 125–26, 134; risk in, 119, 126–27, 129, 130, 150–51; self-interest in, 88, 117, 127–28, 146–47, 150; and sense of debt or obligation, 24, 82–83, 91, 108, 140, 164; and spirit of mercy, 135, 141–42

Girard, René, 165

Godparents as friends, 57

Godsibs, 11, 78–79

Goethe, Johann Wolfgang von, 51, 156

Goldbarth, Albert, 113

Greeley, Andrew, 114

Guests and hospitality, 20–23, 157

Guilt tactics in *The Merchant of Venice*, 145–49

Hans, James, 35–36

Happiness, attainment of, 80

Hartrup, Willard W., 86

Hass, Robert, 103–4, 109

Hecht, Anthony, 61

Hellman, Lillian, 68–70, 97–99, 102

Hemingway, Ernest, 15, 17, 65–67

Henry, O., 160

Herodotus, 159

Hofmannsthal, Hugo von, 83

Holland, Lady Saba, 50

Homosexuality: as issue in friendship, 66–77, 158, 159; as issue in *The Merchant of Venice*, 121, 142–45, 165

Hospitality and friendship, 20–23, 157

Hutter, Horst, 155

Hyde, Lewis, 9, 83–86, 88–89, 92–93, 96–97, 103, 109, 115, 117, 124, 130, 133, 134, 150, 159–60

Ibsen, Henrik, 120

Idealization of friendship, 120

Identity: influence of friends upon, 35

Imaginary friends, 2

Immortality through friendship, 101–9

Indirection: and expression of intimacy, 62–64; and gift giving, 98, 108, 124, 136, 137

Inscriptions, expression of affection in, 58–59

Insults: as game of friendship, 41–43, 157

Intimacy: concealment as agent for, 55–56; effects of pressures for, 64; and privacy, 55, 90–91

Invitations: as courting of friends, 14, 158

Invocation of names of friends: as literary device, 59–62

Irving, John, 7

James, Alice, 159

Jarrell, Randall, 60, 158

Jewett, Sarah Orne, 160

Johnson, Samuel, 9, 37–38, 40, 44, 91–92, 140

Joking in friendships, 41–42; and importance of amusement, 38–39

Joubert, Joseph, 29

Joys, sharing of, 44–45; envy in, 45; and gift giving, 92; gloating in, 45, 46

Justice: and friendship, 165; and mercy, 141–42

Kafka, Franz, 3
Kaplan, Justin, 159
Keats, John, 20, 156, 162
Kennedy, Rose, 55
Keohane, Nannerl O., 162
Kirsch, Arthur, 151, 165
Knowles, John, 102
Kula: as ceremonial gift exchange, 97

Lamb, Charles, 120–21
Language and gestures in friendships, 39–40
La Rochefoucauld, 44, 110, 162
Laughter in friendships, 38–39
Lawrence, D. H., 158
Lee, Susan, 67
Lepp, Ignace, 162
Lévi-Strauss, Claude, 159, 163
Lewis, C. S., 36, 70, 156, 157, 163
Lindsey, Karen, 159
London, Jack, 58
Loneliness and alienation, 3–4; and functions of friendship, 114
Love: compared to friendship, 158–59; and conflicts with friendship, 164
Lowell, Robert, 60, 157–58
Luther, Martin, 113
Lyly, John, 163

Male-female friendships, 73, 137, 159, 162
Male friendships: affection expressed in, 63–64, 65–67, 156; bonding in, 158
Malraux, André, 116
Malory, Sir Thomas, 43
Market or commodity exchange: compared to gifts, 84–86, 88, 161
Marriage: effect on friendship, 120; and freedom of action, 152
Martial, 118
Martin, Robert, 74–75, 77

Massim tribes, gift exchange in, 97
Maupassant, Guy de, 157
Mauss, Marcel, 159, 164
Meal sharing: and business activities, 160–61; in reunions, 156; as ritual, 19–22
Meilaender, Gilbert C., 114–15, 141, 146, 164, 165
Merchant of Venice, The, 24, 97, 113, 118–54, 163–65; conversion of Shylock in, 133–34; gift giving in, 122–42; guilt tactics in, 145–49; issue of homosexuality in, 121, 142–45; mercy and justice in, 135, 141–42; ring trick in, 128–30; usury in, 124–25, 132–33
Mercy and gift giving, 135, 141–42
Midgley, Graham, 142, 163
Mill, John Stuart, 80, 81
Miller, Henry, 160
Miller, Jean Baker, 161
Mills, Laurens J., 163
Milton, John, 82–83, 103
Misfortune, sharing of, 44–45, 55
Molière, 160
Money: and effect on friendship, 163
Montaigne, Michel de, 90–91, 92, 95–97, 99–100, 102, 110
Montesquieu, Baron de, 110
Morris, Colin, 71, 111
Morrison, Toni, 102, 161
Morse, Fanny, 159
Motives for friendship, 5, 53–54, 80
Movies, friendship in, 5–6
Mulder, Mab Lohuizen, 162
Musgrove, Jeannie Field, 90
Myerhoff, Barbara, 104–9

Names, exchange of, 57–58, 157
Napoleon, 112
Nelson, Benjamin, 113, 132, 145, 163

Networks and support systems, 46–52
Nietzsche, Friedrich, 21, 26, 45, 46, 73, 127–128, 160
Nin, Anaïs, 156
Nixon, Richard, 109
Number of friendships: conflicts concerning, 95–96
Nzema men, friendship among, 77

Oates, Joyce Carol, 1
Obligations: fear of, 23–24; in gitt exchange, 24, 82–83, 91, 108, 140, 164; in marriage, 152
Openness and frankness: effects of, 29, 30; lack of, 54–56; and pressures for intimacy, 64
Opie, Iona and Peter, 14, 64

Paine, Robert, 156
Parting of friends, 16–18
Pascal, Blaise, 30
Perry, Ralph Burton, 156
Piercy, Marge, 59
Plato, 7
Play. *See* Games and play
Plutarch, 30, 95, 96, 160, 161
Pound, Ezra, 16, 18, 20, 21, 26
Privacy and intimacy, 55, 90–91
Puritan heritage: and aversion to ritual, 12, 23
Pynchon, Thomas, 4
Pythias and Damon, 110–11

Racine, Jean, 73–74
Rader, Rosemary, 159
Raleigh, Walter, 163
Reciprocation in gift giving, 161; and sense of debt or obligation, 24, 82–83, 91, 108, 140, 164
Reductive analysis of friendship, 5, 53–54
Relaxation and excitement in friendship, 37–38

Religious aspects of friendship, 12, 23, 111–17
Residual forms for cultivating friendship, 78, 79
Reunion of friends, 18–20; function of meals in, 156
Revenge and mercy, 141
Reynolds, Vernon, 160
Rich, Adrienne, 60
Risk taking in gift giving, 119, 126–27, 129, 130, 150–51
Ritual activities: in adolescence, 14–16; aversion to, 12, 23; in childhood, 14; compared to play and games, 36–37; and exchange of names, 57–58; exotic, 11, 78; in friendship, 12; in meal sharing, 19–22; residual equivalents of, 78
Rivalry in friendships, 43
Rockefeller, John D., 161
Rougemont, Denis de, 162
Roux, Joseph, 73

Sacrifice and friendship, 110–11, 116, 119, 145–46, 150, 152
Sahlins, Marshall, 159
Santayana, George, 23–24
Schiller, Friedrich, 36
Schloss, David, 61
Schultz, Philip, 20, 63
Schwartz, Delmore, 60
Scott, Nathan, 115–16, 117
Secrecy: effect on friendship, 54–56
Selden, John, 156
Self: concepts of, 26; inner core of, 26, 28, 81; presentation of, 16
Self-interest: and compassion, 52–53; in friendship, 54; in gift giving, 88, 117, 127–28, 146–47, 150
Seneca, 122
Sentimentality, 49–50, 54; and attitudes toward friendship,

5, 119–20, 146–47; conventions in, 50–51; fear of, 6–7
Separation: and contact with friends, 32–33; and creation of closeness by distance, 56, 162; and parting of friends, 16–18; and reunion of friends, 18–20
Sex: as subject of literature, 155
Sexual differences in friendship, 63–77
Sexuality: and celibate cohabitation, 159; and conventional sexual roles, 143–45; current discourses on, 155; and faithfulness in marriage, 152. *See also* Homosexuality
Shakespeare, William: *Henry IV*, part 1, 38–39; *Hamlet*, 27, 101–2; *King Lear*, 83; *The Merchant of Venice*, 24, 97, 113, 118–54; *The Taming of the Shrew*, 39
Shaw, Irwin, 160
Shell, Marc, 132, 151, 164
Sincerity, 27, 49, 80–81
Smith-Rosenberg, Carroll, 71–73, 90, 159
Society: effects on friendship, 155–56
Socrates, 7
Solzhenitsyn, Aleksandr, 102, 157
Sophocles, 156
Southwell, Robert, 162
Spiritual usury, 164
Spirituality and friendship, 111–17
Steiner, George, 157
Stevenson, Robert Louis, 35
Strouse, Jean, 159
Success of friends, reactions to, 45–46
Support systems and networks, 46–52

Taboos: against being offended, 41–42; on male expressions of affection, 67
Teasing of friends, 42–43
Telephone and maintenance of friendships, 33
Television shows, friendship in, 5, 6, 156
Therapeutic function of encounter groups, 25–26
Thoreau, Henry D., 81, 112
Thought processes: stimulation by friendship, 38
Tiger, Lionel, 158
Tocqueville, Alexis de, 11, 12, 155
Tovey, Barbara, 145, 146, 148, 149, 163
Trading: connection to friendship, 87
Trilling, Lionel, 25, 26, 27, 39, 80
Twain, Mark, 150, 163

Uhlman, Fred, 14–15, 29, 103
Universality of friendship, 2
Usury: of love, 164; as metaphor for love, 134–35; in *The Merchant of Venice*, 124–25, 132–33; spiritual, 164
Utility, friendship of, 88, 94

Valerius Maximus, 111
Van Doren, Mark, 160
Virtue, friendship of, 88, 94
Voltaire, François Marie Arouet de, 112

Walcott, Derek, 59
Waugh, Evelyn, 38
Whitman, Walt, 74–77, 159
Wiesel, Elie, 100, 157
Wilde, Oscar, 80
Wilson, Thomas, 125, 135
Wister, Sarah, 90
Women. *See* Female friendships
Wordsworth, William, 37, 62, 104
Writing about friendship, decline in, 4, 6

Ronald A. Sharp is Professor of English and Chairman of the English department at Kenyon College. Author of *Keats, Skepticism, and the Religion of Beauty,* as well as numerous translations, reviews, and articles ranging from Shakespeare to modern poetry, he was the first editor of the new series of *The Kenyon Review.*

Library of Congress Cataloging-in-Publication Data
Sharp, Ronald A.
Friendship and literature.
Bibliography: p.
Includes index.
1. Friendship in literature.   I. Title.
PN56.F74S53   1986   809'.93353   86-2102
ISBN 0-8223-0580-1